The
Holy Land

The Land of Jesus

Palphot

Acknowledgements:
We are grateful to all those who assisted in the publication of this up-to-date book:
Photographers, Publishers, The Israel Museum, Jerusalem, The Tower of David Museum,
The Israel Department of Antiquities, The Holyland Corporation, Jerusalem.
The Nature Reserves Authority and other Museums and Institutions.

Photography:
Garo Nalbandian - Hanan Isachar - A. Shabataev
L. Borodulin - S. Mendrea - D. Tal & M. Haramaty
A. Nezer - J. Sahar - Dr. D. Darom - Itamar Grinberg
W. Braun - Z. Radovan - R. Nowitz - M. Tal - Z. Mautner
Osku Puukila - D. Harris - E. Ne'eman

Maps:
Evgeny Barashkov

Drawings:
H. Ron - Andromeda

ISBN 965-280-103-8

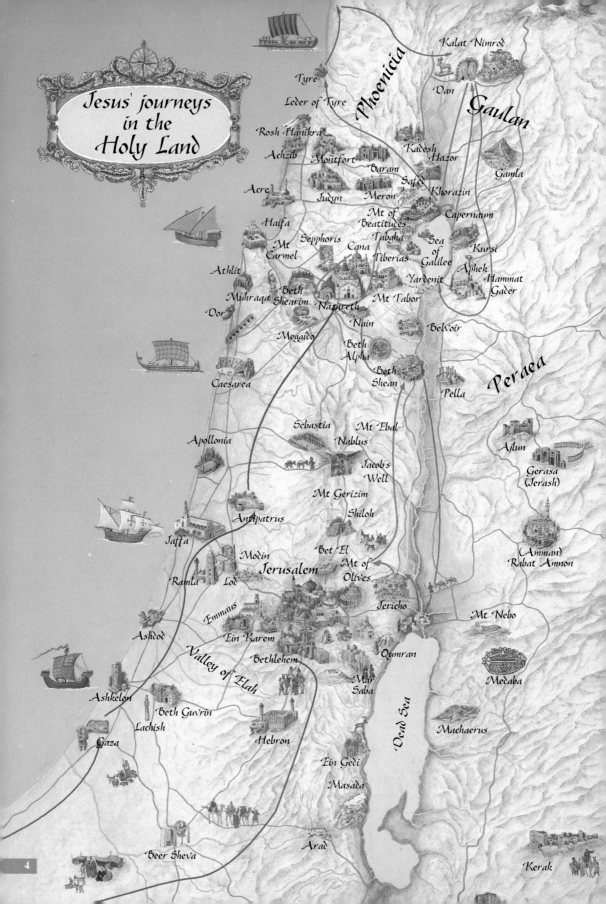

Jesus' journeys
in the
Holy Land

Kalat Nimrod
Phoenicia
Tyre
Leder of Tyre
Dan
Gaulan
Rosh Hanikra
Achziv
Kadesh
Hazor
Montfort
Baram
Gamla
Safed
Acre
Judyn
Meron
Khorazin
Haifa
Mt of
Beatitudes
Capernaum
Mt
Carmel
Sepphoris
Cana
Tabaha
Kursi
Athlit
Beth
Shearim
Cana
Tiberias
Sea
of
Galilee
Aphek
Muhraqa
Nazareth
Yardenit
Hammat
Gader
Dor
Mt Tabor
Megiddo
Nain
Belvoir
Caesarea
Beth
Alpha
Beth
Shean
Pella
Peraea
Sebastia
Mt Ebal
Apollonia
Nablus
Ajlun
Jacob's
Well
Gerasa
(Jerash)
Mt Gerizim
Antipatrus
Shiloh
Jaffa
Bet El
(Amman)
Rabat Ammon
Modin
Jerusalem
Mt of
Olives
Ramla
Lod
Emmaus
Jericho
Mt Nebo
Ashdod
Ein Karem
Bethlehem
Qumran
Valley of Elah
Medaba
Ashkelon
Mar
Saba
Beth Guvrin
Lachish
Dead Sea
Machaerus
Gaza
Hebron
Ein Gedi
Masada
Beer Sheva
Arad
Kerak

Introduction

It is every believer's dream to visit the Land of the Bible, the cradle of the three great monotheistic religions. It was here that Jesus was born, held His ministry, performed His miracles and suffered the Final Agony. No other single person throughout history has so decisively affected the lives of so many people; indeed, the events of His life have repercussions still echoing down the ages.

The Holy Land has been a coveted prize since the beginning of recorded time and many archaeological artifacts from prehistoric times have been discovered here. Its fertility and strategic position attracted the Canaanite tribes who displaced the earliest agriculturalists some five thousand years ago, then the Hebrews, who united the country to form a strong kingdom in about 1000 B.C. Situated across the lines of communication between the great empires of antiquity, it was often overrun. In turn, Assyria, Egypt, Babylon, Greece, Rome and Byzantia assumed control. For a brief period, the Persians held sway but were soon ousted by the Byzantines followed by the Moslems who ruled for over 400 years. Then came the Crusaders, the Mamelukes, the Turks and the British. The Via Maris, the coastal route which passes through

the land, was utilized for military campaigns or peaceful commerce depending on the political climate of the day.

No book in the history of mankind can compare with the Bible as a guide to the history and geography of the Holy Land and archaeological investigations have proved many events which previously passed for stories to be historical. We read how 4000 years ago Abraham journeyed southwards with his wife Sarah, his household, flocks and herds, from Mesopotamia to the Land of Canaan, where the Canaanites lived in a loosely-knit system of city-states. One of these was Salem, or Jerusalem, where Abraham was welcomed by the king who "brought forth bread and wine" (Genesis 14:18). The Bible goes on to relate the story of Abraham's descendants, and the family mausoleum can still be seen in Hebron; we read of the Exodus; of Joshua crossing the River Jordan, and of his many conquests including those of Jericho, Hatzor and Megiddo.

The period of the Judges is vividly described with Samson playing a dramatic role in the Philistine cities of Gaza, Ashdod and Ashkelon and the prophet Samuel anointing Saul king over all Israel. David brought the Holy Ark to Jerusalem, making it his capital, and here his son Solomon built the first Temple. Under Solomon's son, Rehoboam, a revolt resulted in the division of the country into the kingdoms of Israel, comprising ten tribes, and the kingdom of Judah, incorporating the remaining two tribes, with Jerusalem as their capital. Israel survived until 721 B.C., when it was conquered by the Assyrians and the Ten Tribes were lost. Judah survived until 586 B.C., when it fell to Babylon and the Jews were taken into exile. The benevolent Persians allowed them to return to Zion under Ezra and Nehemiah and a new temple arose on

the ruins of the first. The land was absorbed into the Persian empire which was conquered by Alexander the Great in 332 B.C. At first benign, Greek rule later became so oppressive that the Jews rebelled, led by the Maccabees. Independence was achieved in 165 B.C. and the sacred altar rededicated, an event commemorated by Hanukkah, the Feast of Lights.

The Hasmoneans governed for over a hundred years but in 40 B.C., the Romans appointed as puppet king Herod, nominally a Jew, a man whose abnormal personality expressed itself in a lust for power, extreme cruelty and a mania for building. The Romans considered him a friend and granted him rule over most of the historic Land of Israel, including parts of Transjordan. Herod the Great was responsible for the rebuilding of Jerusalem and the Temple as Jesus knew them. He also founded the city of Caesarea, and built Samaria, Herodium and the fortress of Masada on the Dead Sea. After Herod's death in 4 B.C., Palestine came under undisputed Roman rule by a succession of procurators whose seat was in Caesarea. At this time, the Jews were divided into many different groups and sects. There were two main groups, the Pharisees, who were mainly concerned with accurate interpretation of the law, and the Saducees, who were the party of the wealthy priests and aristocracy and controlled Temple worship. The most well-known sects were the Essenes, an ascetic community associated with the Dead Sea Scrolls, and the Zealots, extreme revolutionaries who advocated armed struggle against the Romans. The Samaritans were no longer considered Jews though they shared with them many beliefs. Many of the procurators were incompetent and corrupt and there were frequent disturbances.

According to Christian tradition, the birth of Jesus was foreseen in Old Testament prophecies by Isaiah (7:14,11:1) and Micah (5:2) : "Behold a virgin

shall conceive, and bear a son". It was towards the end of Herod's reign, in around 6 B.C., that Jesus was born to Mary in Bethlehem. The Gospels tell us of the life of Jesus, however since the four Evangelists wrote independently and selectively, we do not have a complete chronological biography. Matthew reports that Herod saw the birth as a threat to his own power, and not only did he seek to kill Jesus, but ordered the massacre of all male children under two. Joseph fled with Mary and Jesus to Egypt, where they remained until the death of Herod. They then went to live in Nazareth and the only episode from Jesus' childhood that is described is the celebration of Passover in Jerusalem. We know that Jesus began His public ministry when he was about thirty years of age, and was baptized by John the Baptist "to fulfil all righteousness" (Matthew 4) in around 29 A.D. His ministry lasted for about three years. However, the New Testament does not give details of dates for the miracles and other events. Even the date of the Crucifixion is in dispute, and we know only that He was crucified and placed in His tomb on a Friday in the Jewish month of Nissan. He was resurrected on the following Sunday, and then ascended to heaven.

Jesus' prophecy that in Jerusalem the enemy "shall not leave one stone upon another" (Luke 19:44) came to pass in 70 A.D. when during the Jewish Revolt, the Roman general Titus razed Jerusalem and the Temple. Some of the Jews who managed to escape set up centers of learning at Yavne, while others, like the defenders of Masada, held out for three more years. Later, in 135, Jewish zealots who attempted to revolt under Simon Bar Kochba were massacred. As Roman power declined that of Byzantia grew, particularly when Christianity was adopted as the official religion of the Empire by Constantine and his mother, Queen Helena. In 326, Helena visited Jerusalem and erected

churches and chapels on sacred sites such as the Church of the Holy Sepulcher, the Eleona on the Mount of Olives, the Church of the Nativity in Bethlehem and the basilica at Abraham's Oak near Hebron, initiating a period of material prosperity in a flourishing Palestine.

Suddenly, a veritable whirlwind arose from the town of Mecca in Saudi Arabia, where Mohammed proclaimed a new religion - Islam. Mohammed mobilized troops to force conversion to Islam. By 634, the Byzantine army south of the Sea of Galilee was crushed, and within a few years Palestine was overrun. Until 1099 it remained under Moslem domination; then, the Crusaders stormed in from the sea and captured Jerusalem in one of the bloodiest battles in recorded history. Jerusalem's two great mosques were turned into headquarters of the Order of the Templars and a church. The Crusaders proceeded to conquer the land, and under their efficient rule from the Kingdom of Jerusalem, prospered for almost a century until in 1187, Saladin, at the head of a Moslem army, destroyed the Crusader army at the Horns of Hittin near the Sea of Galilee.

The Crusaders lost their last foothold in the Holy Land when Acre fell in 1291, and until 1516, when Palestine became part of the Turkish Empire, it was at the mercy of the Mameluke invaders. Turkish sovereignty, too, was largely a story of neglect and indifference under which the country suffered for four hundred years as a provincial backwater. Even pilgrimage was reduced to a trickle. However, the Mamelukes did leave some architectural gems in the Old City of Jerusalem, while the Turkish sultan, Suleiman the Magnificent, constructed the imposing walls around the city. With the opening of the Suez Canal in 1869, the region again grew in importance as a trade route. At the end of the First World War, Britain took control of Palestine from the Turks.

In 1948 Israel was established as a state, and the surrounding Arab nations invaded. Despite their overwhelming superiority in numbers and arms, they were beaten back by the Israel army and an armistice was signed. In the Six-Day War of 1967, the West Bank of the Jordan, including East Jerusalem and the Sinai peninsula came under Israeli control. Following the Yom Kippur War, the Camp David accords brought peace between Egypt and Israel in 1979 and a peace treaty was signed with Jordan in 1994. However, although some agreements have been signed between Israel and the Palestinians, many problems remain unresolved.

We hope and pray that the new millennium will bring peace and will bring to pass the prophecy of Isaiah 2:4 that "they shall beat their swords into plowshares, and their spears into pruninghooks; nation shall not lift up sword against nation, neither shall they learn war any more."

Nazareth

"...The angel Gabriel was sent from God unto a city of Galilee named Nazareth.....And the angel ...said unto her, Fear not Mary: for thou has found favour with God. And, behold, thou shalt conceive in thy womb, and bring forth a son, and shalt call his name Jesus."

Luke 1:26-31

Nazareth, where Jesus spent his childhood, is situated in the Galilean hills overlooking the Jezreel valley. Its winding, cobbled lanes, churches, convents and monasteries, and the all-pervading sense of history vividly conjure up the story of 2000 years ago when Joseph, heeding the angel's words, "took the young child and his mother...and came and dwelt in a city called Nazareth" (Matthew 2:21-23).

Jesus spent his childhood here, though the gospels give no description of these formative years.

Nazareth is not mentioned in the Old Testament and only archaeological evidence points to a village inhabited during the First Temple period. Its Jewish community was almost wiped out by the Romans during the Jewish revolt. Later, with the strengthening of the Roman Empire, the number of Christians grew. From the fourth century, churches were built on the sites which were connected with Jesus and the Virgin Mary.

Today, the population consists of Christians, represented by several denominations, Moslems and Jews. There are many churches, monasteries, convents, hostels and schools.

◀ *Nazareth by David Roberts, 1839*

Above: Painting of the Annunciation

Partial view of Nazareth
▼

The Church of the Annunciation

The presbytery ▲

▲ The Grotto,
the holiest area in the
Basilica of the Annunciation

The focal point of Nazareth is the Church of the Annunciation, situated in the city's old market quarter. This church was completed in 1969 and is the fifth church built on the spot where the Angel Gabriel appeared to Mary to announce the birth of Jesus. Remains of the first church were discovered during excavations in 1955; the second church was built during the Byzantine period, the third by the Crusaders and the fourth was completed in 1877. The new structure consists of two superimposed churches: a lower crypt preserving the Holy Grotto at the the level of former churches, and an upper level which serves as the city's Catholic parish church. The mosaics in the central hall of the church were donated by Catholic communities from all over the world. The Grotto, where the Holy Family is said to have lived after it returned from Egypt, was carved out of the white rock of the hill in the shape of a small square room. Excavations have revealed a small cistern with inscribed plastered stones. A pair of granite columns in the grotto are reputed to have supernatural powers.

Medieval or romanesque capitals from the Crusaders' church

Torso of a statue of St. Peter holding the church and the key to the "Kingdom of Heaven"

Detail of the Zodiac

Plan of the ruins

Cave-dwelling in the village (Cave of the capitals)

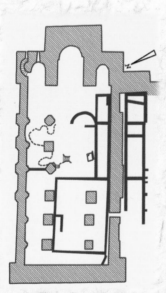

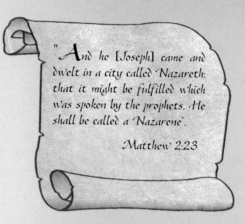

"And he [Joseph] came and dwelt in a city called Nazareth; that it might be fulfilled which was spoken by the prophets, He shall be called a Nazarene".

Matthew 2:23

One of Nazareth's attractions is the Arab souk where people can stop to browse or pick up bargains. There are religious trinkets, beads and other items of jewelry, souvenirs and oriental dresses for the tourist, whilst for the locals there is everything from fresh meat and live chickens to cleaning materials, saucepans and clothes. Part of the fun is the haggling about prices and the variety of types of people to be seen. The souk is particularly lively on Saturdays when the local villagers come into town to trade, along with Jewish families out on a day's excursion. On Fridays the Moslem shops are closed and the Christian shops are closed on Sundays.

◀ *Market scenes in Nazareth*

▼ *Mary's Well*

The Church of St Joseph

Opposite the Church of the Annunciation is the Church of St. Joseph, built over the cave which served as Joseph's carpenty workshop. Another tradition holds that it was the home of the Holy Family. The present church was built by the Custody of the Holy Land over the remains of Byzantine and Crusader churches which can still be seen in the crypt. Beneath the crypt is the Holy Cave and beside it, a water cistern.

Above: The Holy Family

Above right:
The Grotto under the Church
of St. Joseph, with silos

"*And when they had performed all things...they returned into Galilee, to their own city 'Nazareth. And the child grew and waxed strong in spirit, filled with wisdom, and the grace of God was upon him".*

Luke 2:39–40

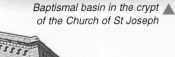

Baptismal basin in the crypt ▲
of the Church of St Joseph

The Church of the Synagogue

From the Gospel, as from later quotations, it is known that at least until the 6th century, Nazareth was mainly a Jewish village. The Gospel mentions the synagogue in which Jesus preached his message to his fellow-villagers who were not enthusiastic.

Architectural remains, such as plinths and pillars from a synagogue found in the village, are preserved in the courtyard of the Franciscan friary. Today the pilgrims visit the "synagogue" in a vaulted hall, perhaps from the Crusader period, near the Greek-Catholic church built in 1882.

The Church of St. Gabriel and Mary's Well

According to tradition, the Angel Gabriel first appeared to Mary while she was drawing water from the well, and then Mary went to her home where the Annunciation took place. The Crusaders built a church on the site in the 12th century, and the present church was built by the Greek Orthodox in 1781. Remains of the Crusader church, with its Armenian tiles, can be seen in the crypt.

Throughout its history, there has been only one well in Nazareth. An aqueduct brings the spring water to an ornamental fountain located just below St. Gabriel's Church.

▼ *Mount of Precipitation*

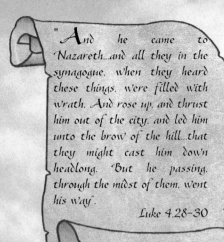

The Mount of Precipitation

South of Nazareth is a mountain associated with the dramatic story described by Luke. Jesus gave a sermon in the synagogue and antagonized the congregants who wanted to hurl him down the hill and kill him. A seventeenth century pilgrim wrote: "Two miles from Nazareth ... one encounters a cliff on the edge of a mountain that both locals and strangers called in ancient times, as they do today, 'the Lord's precipice' ".
Traditionally, he was saved by leaping from this mountain, called the Mount of Precipitation or Mount of the Leap.

Mary's Well in the Church of St. Gabriel ▶

Cana

Cana, near Nazareth, is the site where Jesus performed his first miracle, as related in John 2. At a wedding he was attending, the wine for the sanctification ran out and Jesus ordered that six stone jars used in the ritual purification be filled with water. When drawn off, this miraculously became wine. "This beginning of miracles did Jesus in Cana of Galilee, and manifested forth his glory; and his disciples believed on him."

(John 2:11)

Here are two churches, one Greek Orthodox, and the other, which is Franciscan, was built in 1879 on the remains of a 6th century sanctuary. This was the site of the village synagogue where the wedding is believed to have taken place. In

▲ *Interior of the Church of the Miracle*

The Greek Orthodox and Melchite Churches ▼

the crypt is an ancient pitcher reputed to be a replica of one of the six original jars. Another chapel, of St. Bartholomew, is dedicated to Nathaniel, a native of Cana who was initially skeptical of Jesus and said "can anything good come out of Nazareth?"
(John 1:46).

Excavations have revealed that the Church had indeed been erected on the ruins of a synagogue. An inscription of a dedication written in Aramaic was found buried in the mosaic floor: "This is to honor the memory of Joseph, son of Tanhum son of Butah and his sons who made this mosaic. May he be blessed, Amen".

"On the third day there was a marriage at Cana in Galilee, and the mother of Jesus was there: Jesus also was invited to the marriage with his disciples".

John 2: 1-2

Above:
The Greek Orthodox Church
The crypt in the Church of the Miracle, with the Jar
Painting showing Jesus at the wedding ▼
in Cana, in the Church of the Miracle

Mount Tabor

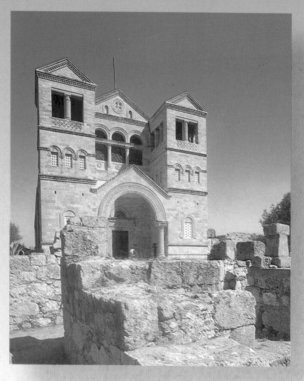

Mount Tabor, at 1850 feet, is the highest mountain in the area. From here there is a magnificent view of the Jezreel plain and Nazareth to the west, Samaria to the south and the Galilee to the north. The top is a large plateau.

It was traditionally on the summit of Mount Tabor, "the high mountain apart", that Jesus was transfigured in the eyes of Peter, James and John "and his face did shine as the sun, and his raiment was white as the light" (Matthew 17:2).

*The Basilica of the Transfiguration
Mount Tabor*

"*And Jesus taketh with him Peter, and James, and John, and leadeth them up into an high mountain apart by themselves: and he was transfigured before them*".

Mark 9:2

In the time of the Judges, at the judge Deborah"s behest, "Barak went down from Mount Tabor and ten thousand men after him" (Judges 4:14) to fight Jabin, King of Hazor. This was one of the first large battles fought by the Israelites during their conquest of the land from the Canaanites. They were based at this strategic point and Sisera, with his 900 chariots, was unable to attack them uphill. In the end, the enemy got stuck in the mud and was completely routed. Josephus Flavius, who for a time commanded the Jewish forces in

Interior of the Basilica of the Transfiguration ▲▼

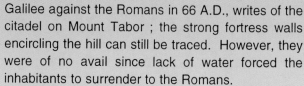
Galilee against the Romans in 66 A.D., writes of the citadel on Mount Tabor ; the strong fortress walls encircling the hill can still be traced. However, they were of no avail since lack of water forced the inhabitants to surrender to the Romans.

The first churches were built here around 400 A.D. In the time of the Crusaders, a strongly fortified monastery was built by the Benedictines which managed to withstand attacks by Saladin. However, after the defeat at the Horns of Hittin in 1187, the monks were forced to abandon the site. Sultan Beybars later demolished all the buildings and only in the seventeenth century was the site resettled, this time by Franciscans, who hold it to this day.

The Greek Orthodox Church of St. Elias was built on the foundations of a Crusader building in 1911. In 1924, Antonio Barluzzi's Basilica of the Transfiguration was consecrated. Among its outstanding

▲ *Tympan from the fourth century Basilica on Mount Tabor.*

◀ *The Chapel of the Catacomb in the Greek Orthodox church*

Aerial view of Mt. Tabor with the Basilica of the Transfiguration on the left and the Greek Orthodox church on the right
▼

Statue of His Holiness Pope Paul VI who visited the Holy Land.
▶

▲ **Nain** - *A little over 3 kilometers south of Mt. Tabor is the peaceful village of Nain ("Beauty"). Here Jesus performed the miracle of restoring the widow's son to life.*
Luke 7:11-15

features is its facade of two massive towers linked by a large Byzantine-style arch. The interior is divided by three pillars into naves, the central one terminating in a semicircular apse. The dome of the apse features a lovely mosaic depicting the transfiguration. The Church encloses three chapels which commemorate Peter's proposal to build three tabernacles, one each for Jesus, Moses and Elijah. The Grotto of Christ is at the eastern end of the church and the Elijah and Moses chapels are located in the towers. In addition to the Basilica, the Franciscans have built a large monastery and a hospice.

The present church built on the ruins of the Byzantine and Crusader churches ▶

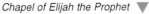

Chapel of Moses ▼

Chapel of Elijah the Prophet ▼

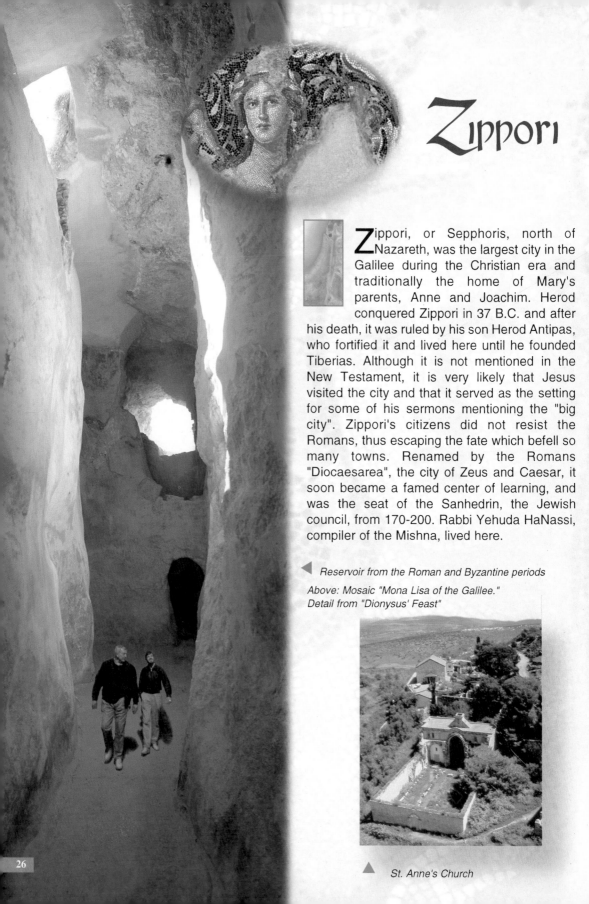

Zippori

Zippori, or Sepphoris, north of Nazareth, was the largest city in the Galilee during the Christian era and traditionally the home of Mary's parents, Anne and Joachim. Herod conquered Zippori in 37 B.C. and after his death, it was ruled by his son Herod Antipas, who fortified it and lived here until he founded Tiberias. Although it is not mentioned in the New Testament, it is very likely that Jesus visited the city and that it served as the setting for some of his sermons mentioning the "big city". Zippori's citizens did not resist the Romans, thus escaping the fate which befell so many towns. Renamed by the Romans "Diocaesarea", the city of Zeus and Caesar, it soon became a famed center of learning, and was the seat of the Sanhedrin, the Jewish council, from 170-200. Rabbi Yehuda HaNassi, compiler of the Mishna, lived here.

◀ *Reservoir from the Roman and Byzantine periods*

Above: Mosaic "Mona Lisa of the Galilee."
Detail from "Dionysus' Feast"

▲ *St. Anne's Church*

A Crusader fortress built on top of an earlier Roman building crowns the hill, while nearby a 4000 seat Roman amphitheater, streets, a water system, public buildings, houses and other structures from the Roman and Byzantine periods, have been unearthed. A number of magnificent mosaics have been uncovered including one in a reconstructed Roman villa, and a Dionysian mosaic floor with a woman's face, known as the "Mona Lisa of the Galilee".

Flowers of Galilee ▶

▼
The Crusaders' citadel,
which today serves as the Visitors' Center

Tiberias

On the south-western edge of the Sea of Galilee is Tiberias, capital of the Lower Galilee It was founded around 20 A.D by Herod Antipas, son of Herod the Great, on the site of ancient Rakkath, mentioned in Joshua 19:35 as a fenced city, together with Hammath and Kinneret. Planned in the Greek style, it was independent and allowed to formulate its own laws and mint its own coins. In 67 it surrendered peaceably to the Romans. With the fall of Jerusalem three years later, Jews flocked to Tiberias and schools of religious learning were set up. The Sanhedrin moved here from Sepphoris and here the Jerusalem Talmud, which contains Biblical criticism, commentary and tradition, was compiled.

Tiberias, together with Jerusalem, Hebron and Safed, became one of the four holy cities of Palestine. Christianity spread in Tiberias only under the late Byzantines in the sixth century. The city was conquered by the Arabs in 636 A.D, then by the Crusaders who remained from 1100 to 1247, using it as an administrative center. It declined thereafter and only began to grow again in the eighteenth century. The walls of black basalt are from the times of the Crusaders, though they were restored by the Bedouin chief Daher el-Amar in 1738. The great Spanish twelfth century philosopher and physician, Maimonides, was buried here in 1204, and his tomb is still visited by many pilgrims.

The hot mineral springs south of Tiberias make it a health-giving spa, as popular today as it was with the Roman officials and their families nearly 2000 years ago.

▲ *The church on the hill of Bereniki*

▼ *Partial view of modern Tiberias*

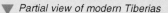

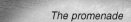
The promenade

Mount Arbel

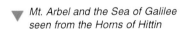On the western shore of the Sea of Galilee are the towering cliffs of Mount Arbel, referred to in Hosea 10:14 as the "battlefield of Beit-arbel". Here, in 39 B.C., Herod launched an all-out campaign against the Zealots who had entrenched themselves in the caves, and Josephus tells the tragic story of a father who killed his seven children, his wife and himself rather than be taken captive.

Mt. Arbel with the Sea of Galilee ▶

▼ *Mt. Arbel and the Sea of Galilee seen from the Horns of Hittin*

Sea of Galilee

The Sea of Galilee is the catchment basin for the Jordan River and is fed by the melting snows of Mount Hermon to the north. Numerous other seasonal streams flow down from the surrounding mountains to this low-lying, fresh-water lake, 685 feet below sea level.

The Sea of Galilee is in fact a lake, it is 13 miles long and 7.5 miles wide, 50 meters deep, with a surface area of 63.7 square miles. In a land so barren, this fresh-water lake provides much needed greenery, respite for the eyes and the soul and, through the intense cultivation possible here, nourishment for the body. "One may call this place the ambition of nature», wrote

▼ *Pilgrim's boats on the Sea of Galilee*

Josephus, «where it forces those plants that are naturally enemies to one another to agree together". Sometimes, however, there are sudden violent storms as described by Matthew: "There arose a great tempest in the sea, insomuch that the ship was covered with the waves" (Matthew 8:24).

The ancients waxed poetic when they named the lake. They called it Kinneret, which means "lyre", because its shape reminded them of that musical instrument played by King David and by the Levites in the Temple. The lake lies deep in a crevice created by earthquakes. Those same earth movements resulted in the appearance of hot sulfur springs around the shore, to which for centuries the ill have flocked to be cured of their maladies.

Jesus spent most of his three-year public ministry in towns and villages around the Sea of Galilee. Some scholars, taking note of the large number of sick people that came to Jesus to be healed, believe that they may have initially come to the region to take advantage of the hot springs.

The Galilee boat - now preserved and housed in a museum

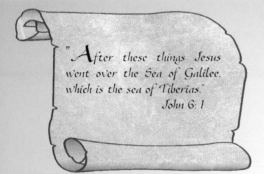

"After these things Jesus went over the Sea of Galilee, which is the sea of Tiberias."

John 6: 1

Tabgha

The name Tabgha is a distortion of the Greek word Heptapegon, which means "Seven Springs" ; in the past, seven springs met at this point and flowed into the Sea of Galilee, however today only five remain. This is the traditional site of the Miracle of the Loaves and Fishes. The Gospels tell how five thousand people gathered to hear Jesus' words and stayed until nightfall. "Give ye them to eat", said Jesus to his apostles. They answered, "We have no more but five loaves and two fishes" (Luke 9:13). Jesus blessed the food and it sufficed for all. The table rock where this wonder took place has been the altar of successive churches, the earliest built in the fourth century and replaced a century later

▼ *The exterior of the Church of the Multiplication of the Loaves and the Fishes*

ENTRY

by a larger structure. The mosaic pavement still remains in the modern church, which was built in 1982 for the German Benedictines in Byzantine style. The mosaic in front of the altar symbolizes the loaves and fishes and in the transept are beautiful mosaics depicting water birds and plants.

"*Then he took the five loaves and the two fishes. and looking up to heaven. he blessed them...and gave to the disciples to set before the multitude. And they did eat and were all filled.*"

Luke 9:16-17

▼ *The interior of the Church of the Multiplication*

The Sanctuary
at the Church
of the Multiplication
of the Loaves and Fishes

Part of the Byzantine
mosaic floor

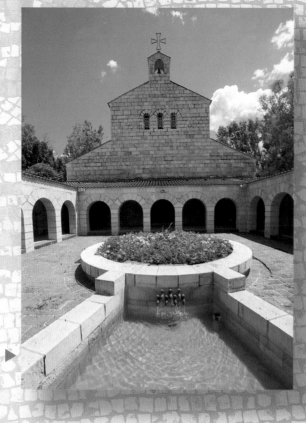

▲ The Sea of Galilee boat shown here is based partly on a mosaic that dates from the 1st century AD and was found near the Sea of Galilee. The boats used by Jesus' followers would have been about 24 feet long.

"*He entered into a ship with his disciples, and came into the parts of Dalmanutha*".

Mark 8: 10

The courtyard of the Church of Multiplication of the Loaves and Fishes ▶

▼ Dalmanutha prayer site, on the western side of the Sea of Galilee

Church of St Peter's Primacy

Nearby, along the shore, is the Church of St. Peter's Primacy, or Mensa Christi - the Table of Christ. This simple chapel marks the place where Jesus, after the resurrection, "showed himself again to his disciples at the sea of Tiberias" (John 21:1), and they ate together. The rock emerging from the center of the floor is the "table" at which they ate. Jesus then appointed Simon Peter to the office of the Primacy with the words "Feed my sheep" (John 21:16). Built by the Franciscans in 1943 on Byzantine foundations, the church is located on a small quay with rock-hewn steps on which Jesus is said to have stood as he looked over the water.

Interior of the Church of St Peter's Primacy

Pilgrims outside the Church of St Peter's Primacy

Statue overlooking the Sea of Galilee. This statue depicts Christ after the Resurrection, appearing for the third time before his disciples

Capernaum

In Roman times; Capernaum was a wealthy Jewish town. The remains of a fourth century white limestone synagogue show that it was the most elaborate of the early Galilean synagogues, with its soaring columns, decorated ashlars and its inscribed pillars. Here Jesus met his first disciples - Peter, Andrew, James, John and Matthew, all fishermen who worked on the Sea of Galilee. Jesus preached and performed many miracles in Capernaum and the surrounding area. Here he healed Peter's wife's mother of a fever, brought a child back to life, cured a leper, healed the centurion's servant and "he cast out the spirits

Bird's eye view of Capernaum and the Sea of Galilee, showing the family living quarters and the new church covering Peter's house

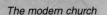

The modern church

with his word and healed all that were sick" (Matthew 8:16). However the people of Capernaum did not believe in Jesus and he consequently cursed them: "And thou, Capernaum, which art exalted unto heaven, shalt be brought down to hell" (Matthew 11:23). The city was destroyed by the Arabs in the seventh century and when the site was acquired by the Franciscans in 1891 it was nothing but a wasteland strewn with engraved stones.

There are two parts to the remains of Capernaum: the section belonging to the Franciscans which was excavated in 1968-84, sponsored by the Italian government, and the Greek Orthodox site which was excavated in 1978-82 by the Israel Department of Antiquities.

The second century synagogue has been partially restored. The synagogue faced Jerusalem and consisted of a rectangular columned basilica with a broad nave and two narrow aisles separated by elegant columns. The interior was plastered and decorated

Model of the house of St. Peter
Interior of the new church

with reliefs. Among the carvings are typical Jewish motifs such as a shofar (ram's horn), menorah (seven-branched candelabrum), star of David and a mobile Ark of the Covenant resembling a Hellenistic temple on wheels. The synagogue had one main and two side entrances and two rows of stone benches, one above the other, running around three sides. There was also a women's gallery. Beneath the floor, excavations have uncovered the remains of a first century synagogue thought to be that in which Jesus preached.

The traditional house of St. Peter, one of a group of houses, was discovered beneath the Byzantine octagonal church, west of the main building, as attested to by graffiti inscriptions on the walls in Aramaic, Greek and Latin. The original building consisted of rooms

▲

Remains of the ancient synagogue on which Jewish symbols are carved. The menorah and the relief of a jug with bunches of grapes can clearly be seen.

▼ *Partial view of the ancient synagogue*

*A relief from the synagogue showing
the carriage for carrying
the Holy Ark of the Covenant.*

around a central courtyard which was later covered over. In the center is a mosaic depicting a peacock. Surrounding the excavations is a park with parts of columns and decorated stones from the ancient buildings.

*Columns of the ancient synagogue, which is probably built on
the site of the original building where Jesus preached*

▲ A relief from the synagogue showing a Star of David

> "And when Jesus was entered into Capernaum, there came unto him a centurion beseeching him, and saying, Lord, my servant lieth at home sick of the palsy...And Jesus saith unto him, I will come and heal him".
>
> Matthew 8:6-7

▲ To the left of the picture is a mill for breaking olives, and to the right an oil press which can also be used to make flour.

The Greek Orthodox Church at Capernaum ▼

Mount of Beatitudes

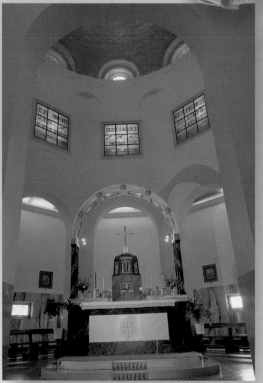

Between Tabgha and Capernaum, on a slight rise, is the Mount of the Beatitudes where Jesus preached the Sermon on the Mount. Remains of a small Byzantine church were discovered here in 1935, but the Franciscans chose to rebuild the modern Church of the Beatitudes on the hill-top, not over the ancient chapel. Constructed by Antonio Barluzzi of local basalt with a colonnade of white stone, the octagonal church recalls the eight blessings which are inscribed on the walls of the octagon, with the ninth inside the dome. There is also a pilgrim hostel - a quiet haven with a magnificent view overlooking the placid waters of the lake.

View of the Sea of Galilee and the Church of the Beatitudes
▼

▲ *The high altar in the Church of the Beatitudes*

"Blessed are the poor in spirit: for theirs is the kingdom of heaven.

Blessed are they that mourn: for they shall be comforted.

Blessed are the meek: for they shall inherit the earth.

Blesssed are they which do hunger and thirst after righteousness: for they shall be filled.

Blessed are the merciful: for they shall obtain mercy.

Blessed are the pure in heart: for they shall see God.

Blessed are the peacemakers: for they shall be called the children of God.

Blessed are they which are persecuted for righteousness' sake: for theirs is the kingdom of heaven.

Blessed are ye, when men shall revile you, and persecute you, and shall say all manner of evil against you falsely, for my sake.

Rejoice, and be exceeding glad: for great is your reward in heaven: for so persecuted they the prophets which were before you.

Matthew 5: 3-12

Korazin

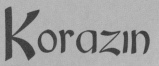

The Jews of the thriving town of Korazin refused to allow Jesus to preach there and Luke 10:13-15 recalls the curse laid upon the unrepentant cities. The site was first excavated in 1905, when the three great portals and a wealth of carved friezes and capitals of the black basalt synagogue were discovered. Later digs unearthed houses, an oil press, streets and ritual baths attached to the synagogue. Korazin seems to have been destroyed by an earthquake in the third century and was never rebuilt.

▲

Remains of the ancient synagogue of Korazin

▼

"*W*oe unto thee Chorazin! woe unto thee Bethsaida! For if the mighty works which were done in you, had been done in Tyre and Sidon, they would have repented long ago in sackcloth and ashes.

Luke 10:13

Kursi & Bethsaida

△ *Church of the Miracle of the Swine, Kursi*

Kursi is the New Testament Gergesa, or Gadara, where Jesus met two men possessed of devils. He miraculously cast the devils out of the men into a herd of swine which stampeded into the water and was drowned. The site of the miracle was a mystery for centuries, until a bulldozer clearing the way for a new road found a Byzantine basilica with a fine mosaic floor. Attached to it was a chapel and fortified monastery, while in a well-preserved barrel-roofed crypt were the skeletons of more than 30 middle-aged males.

▽ *Church of the Miracle of the Swine, Kursi*   △ *View towards Bethsaida*

Yardenit

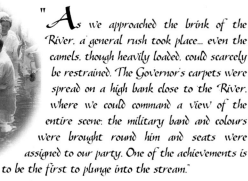

Pilgrims from far and wide come to the Yardenit, the Place of Baptism, to immerse themselves in the holy waters of the River Jordan. The Children of Israel crossed the River Jordan opposite Jericho when they came into the Promised Land (Joshua 3). The prophet Elijah divided its waters and crossed with Elisha on dry land and was then taken by a whirlwind up to Heaven (II Kings 2). Naaman the Syrian dipped in the waters seven times and was cured of his leprosy. And "Jesus [was] baptized of John in Jordan" (Mark 1:9). Jesus' site of baptism was probably further south, near the Judean desert, however due to its position on the Israel-Jordan border, during the Arab-Israel conflict the Yardenit site was developed by Kibbutz Kinnereth and facilities provided for pilgrims wishing to participate in baptism ceremonies.

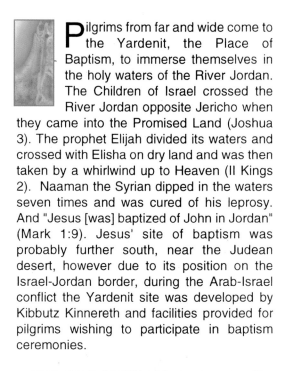

Jordan Valley

From its sources the Dan, Hatzbani and Banias, the River Jordan flows through the Huleh valley and the Sea of Galilee via the Jordan Valley, spilling into the northern end of the Dead Sea. This last tract winds along 103.7 miles although the actual distance is only around 64.6 miles. The northern part of the Jordan valley is lush and fertile with citrus and mango groves, orchards and fishponds. As the River Jordan wends its way south-wards, the land becomes increasingly barren until it reaches the Judean desert.

Naharayim, Israel-Jordan border

Belvoir (Kochav Hayarden)

Set on a scarp rising to 1000 feet above the Jordan Valley is Belvoir, one of the key fortresses of the Crusaders. It is surrounded by a moat 30 feet deep and 60 feet across, and covers an area of 32 acres. The remains of its seven towers, the storerooms, kitchen and dining room can still be seen. The fortress was built around 1138 and was later acquired by the Hospitallers, who held it until they were forced to capitulate to Saladin in 1189. From here there are magnificent views of the Jordan Valley and plain of Jezreel.

Belvoir with the Jordan Valley in the background

Hammat Gader

The warm water lake

Minaret of the Syrian mosque

The hot springs of Hammat Gader were known from biblical times and the Byzantine empress Eudocia, who lived in Jerusalem in the fifth century, claimed they were the best in the Roman world. Hammat Gader is situated at the point where Israel, Jordan and Syria meet, in the Yarmuk valley. Adjacent is a fifth century synagogue floor with many inscriptions in Aramaic and Hebrew.

Nearer the River Yarmuk, the remains of possibly the largest complex of bath-houses in the whole of the Roman empire have been discovered. The bath-houses were built of black and white stone and the impressive remains include the Lepers' Pool, the Oval Pool and a large hall with enormous windows built in the form of an arch. Nearby are modern bathing pools filled with hot spring water at temperatures ranging from 29-51 C. Alligators brought in from Florida bask happily in shallow, enclosed pools.

View of the Roman bath-house

Ein Gev & Jordan Park

▶ Ruins of the ancient town of Susita

Kibbutz Ein Gev on the east bank of the Sea of Galilee was founded in 1937 when the only approach was by sea from Tiberias. Fishing was the main occupation and life was particularly difficult because Syrian soldiers, stationed immediately to the north and east, threatened the daily life and livelihood of the members. Today Ein Gev is prosperous and safe, making a living from its plantations of dates and bananas and a fish restaurant which is "a must" for every tourist.

The beautiful Jordan River Park, with its breathtaking views of the Sea of Galilee and the Golan Heights, is one of Israel's favorite picnic sites.

The Jordan River Park ▶

Kibbutz Ein Gev and the fish restaurant, ▼ with Mt. Susita in the background

Caesarea Philippi

When Jesus and his disciples came to Caesarea Philippi, they found a fruitful glen, through which a rushing river flowed, with opulent residences, colonnaded streets and gigantic temples. The city of Paneas was given to King Herod the Great by the Roman emperor Augustus. As a token of his gratitude, Herod built a palace to Caesar and after his death, Philip, one of his sons, embellished the town and made it his capital, renaming it Caesarea Philippi. It was here that Jesus asked his disciples who the people thought he was. Simon acknowledged Jesus as "the Christ, the Son of the living God" to which Jesus replied "thou art Peter, and upon this rock [Petrus] I will build my church". Jesus gave Peter the keys to the kingdom of heaven saying "whatsoever thou shalt bind on earth shall be bound in heaven: and whatsoever thou shalt loose on earth shall be loosed in heaven" (Matthew 16,18-19). Banias later became important to Christianity and had its own bishop from the fourth to seventh centuries. During the Crusader and Mameluke periods it was a strategic city surrounded by towers and a wall, the remains of which can still be seen today.

The present name dates from the seventh-century Arab conquest and back to the ancient Greek name Panias. Lacking the letter "P" in their alphabet, Arab pronunciation became "Banias".

▲ *Votary niches in the Temple of Pan at Banias*

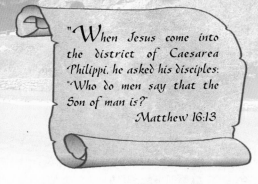

"When Jesus come into the district of Caesarea Philippi, he asked his disciples: "Who do men say that the Son of man is?"

Matthew 16:13

Mount Hermon

Snow-capped Mount Hermon, the highest mountain in the country, lying partly also in Lebanon and Syria, dominates the Golan and north-eastem Galilee. The principal peak, resembling an immense truncated cone, is divided into three summits, the highest rising to a height of 9230 feet, and the rain and snow it receives affect the water supply of the whole region. Psalm 133 praises it: "how good and pleasant it is for brethren to dwell together in unity. It is like... the dew of Hermon". At the time of Joshua's conquest, the majestic Hermon constituted the northem limit of Israel (Joshua 11:3) "which Hermon the Sidonians call Sirion; and the Amorites call it Shenir" (Deut. 3:8-9) It is regarded by some as the "high mountain" (Matt. 17:1) where the Transfiguration took place.

The Hermon is a nature reserve with beautiful flora and many fauna. Israel's only ski site is on the slopes of Mount Hermon and its facilities are operated by the nearby moshav Neve Ativ. Nearby are several Druze villages.

On a spur in the foothills is Castle Nimrod, or Kalat el-Subeiba, a well-preserved fortress wlth round towers and huge underground cisterns. Kalat el-Subeiba was built as a hideout for a peculiar Moslem sect, the Assassins, part of whose life-style was the taking of hashish. In 1129 the castle was given over to King Baldwln II of Jerusalem in return for his protection.

▲ *The Nimrod Fortress*

▼ *Mt. Hermon cable car*

▼ *Mt. Hermon and the Hula Valley*

Golan Heights

The Golan Heights rise high above the Sea of Galilee. Before 1967, from these heights, Syrian troops constantly threatened the peaceful fields and orchards of the kibbutzim below in the Jordan Valley and on the eastern bank of the Lake. These black basalt volcanic mountains, which extend from Mount Hermon in a broad arc east and south to the Yarmuk Valley, were allotted to the half tribe of Manasseh, to whom, according to Deut. 4:43 "they gave Golan in Bashan".

Remains of ancient synagogues have been found in many places on the Golan Heights but perhaps the most moving is that a Gamla where a perfect first century A.D synagogue has been uncovered at the Zealot fortress. When the Romans were approaching in 68 thousands of Gamla's defenders killed themselves and their families rather than be captured.

◄ *Saar brook on the Golan Heights*

▼ *Gamla, the ancient synagogue at the famous
fortress on the Golan Heights*

Hazor was probably the largest of the Canaanite city-states, and strongly resisted the incursions of the Children of Israel. Joshua 11:10 relates how he took Hazor, and smote the king thereof with a sword; for Hazor was the head of all those kingdoms. Joshua then "burnt Hazor with fire" (Joshua 11:11).

Archaeological excavations have brought to light signs of 21 layers of civilization, beginning in the third millennium B.C, but the earliest large settlement dates from the eighteenth-seventeenth centuries. Above this were four Canaanite strata of good-sized towns, sometimes spread over 200 acres, the last of which was destroyed by Joshua around 1250 B.C. Hazor was an important communications center and stronghold during the time of the Canaanites and finds from this period include a royal palace and a number of temples with remarkable stelae and cult objects; here the basalt lion, symbol of Hazor was found. Solomon's city, with massive walls and gates, was razed by the Assyrian Tiglath-Pileser in 732 B.C. Thereafter there were only small settlements on the site. One of the most interesting finds was King Ahab's water supply system, with a broad shaft and stepped tunnel leading down to the water source.

Tel Hazor

▲ *Kadesh, ruins of the ancient temple*

▼ *Tel Hazor, with Kibbutz Ayelet Hashahar in the background*

Hula Valley

The Hula Nature Reserve is the last remnant of the Hula swamps, once teeming with water buffalo and wild boar, turtles and other water creatures, rare fish and wading birds living a primeval existence among the aquatic plants and creepers. In 1883, Jewish settlers began draining the swamps by planting eucalyptus trees, which use large amounts of water. This freed vast tracts of land for cultivation and helped to eradicate malaria from the region. However, since 1994, waters of the Jordan have been diverted to enlarge the Hula Lake in order to conserve wild life, and part of the area has been set aside as a nature reserve.

The Hula marshes and the Golan Heights with snow-covered Mt Hermon in the background

Metulla

◄ The Trumpeldor Memorial at Tel Hai

The small agricultural town of Metulla on the Lebanese border, with its leisurely atmosphere and old-world charm, is a summer refuge for city-dwellers. Since 1976, thousands of Lebanese have come through "the Good Fence", some for medical care, but most are laborers who commute to work in Israel.

Tel Hai

Today a museum, Tel Hai ("Hill of Life") was an agricultural settlement which was attacked by Arabs in 1920. The defence was led by Joseph Trumpeldor, a Russian Jew who had lost his arm in the Tsar's army. During the battle, eight settlers died including Trumpeldor, whose last words were: "It is good to die for our country". The Museum describes life in the early Jewish settlements.

The "Tachanah" waterfall ▼

Metulla, general view with Mount Hermon ▼

The Ari Synagogue ▲

Safed & Meron

High on a mountain-top, more than 3000 feet above sea-level, is Safed, capital of the Upper Galilee. One of the Holy Land's four sacred cities along with Jerusalem, Tiberias and Hebron, Safed is also known as the City of Mysticism, the home of the Kabbala - a medieval philosophy of direct communication between Man and God. The founder and chief exponent of the Kabbala was sixteenth century Rabbi Isaac Luria, also known as Ha'ari, or the Lion. Safed's clean air and combination of wonderful panoramas with narrow, stepped streets and vine-covered courtyards has attracted a colony of sculptors and artists.

Few references to Safed are found before the end of the Second Temple period. Due to its strategic position, it was fortified by Josephus Flavius as one of the key fortresses of the north. Its ruins, upon which the Crusader castle of Saphet was later built,

The old cemetery ▲

Bird's eye view of Safed ▼
with Mt. Meron in the background

can be seen on Citadel Hill, now a municipal park. Within a hundred years of the ousting of the Crusaders, Safed saw an intellectual revival. Its Jews gained reinforcements from the refugees who fled from the Spanish Inquisition, or were expelled from Spain in the fifteenth century, ushering in its Golden Age. Here the first Hebrew printing press in the Middle East was initiated in 1563, greatly advancing the dissemination of learning and language. In the eighteenth century, many Hassidic Jews from Eastern Europe came to settle in Safed. There are many old synagogues belonging to the different sects.

Meron, a small Jewish village founded in 1949, stands on the site of a Talmudic-era settlement with the impressive remains of a second century synagogue. Near Meron are the graves of famous rabbis, notably Rabbi Shimon bar Yohai, a famous Kabbalist and traditional author of the Zohar, the main Kabbalistic work. On the Jewish festival of Lag Ba'omer, a mass pilgrimage is made from Safed to the tomb of Rabbi Shimon. Bonfires are lit and prayers are offered up throughout the night.

The ancient synagogue at Meron ▲

A lane in old Safed ▼

▲ Bird's eye view of Achziv

▲ The cable car

▼ Bird's eye view of Rosh Hanikra

Rosh Hanikra

At Israel's northernmost point, bordering on Lebanon, are the Rosh Hanikra grottoes, where the railway used to pass through a rock-cut tunnel built by the British during World War II. Here the waves churn and roar through the white limestone rock caverns and subterranean passages which they have carved through the ages. The grottoes can be reached by cable-car, though the more adventurous can use the footpath. The caves are accessible in almost any weather, but when the sea is stormy they are even more impressive. From the lookout point there are magnificent views of the rugged coast and the Mediterranean sea. There is no pass through the cliffs and since ancient times when the way led north to the Land of Phoenicia, the ascent has been known as the "Ladder of Tyre", after the first important Phoenician town beyond.

The ancient aqueduct near Nahariya

▲ Nahariya Beach

Monfort

The ruins of the Montfort castle on a high spur, surrounded by natural forest, are the largest in the western Galilee. The fortress was destroyed by Saladin in 1187, shortly after completion. It was then sold to the knights of the Teutonic Order of St. Mary who rebuilt it, but were forced by the Mameluke Sultan Beybars to leave the site in 1271.

Nahariya

Nahariya is a pleasant sea-side resort town with the Gaaton Brook flowing through its central boulevard. Founded in 1934 by immigrants from Nazi-dominated Germany, it soon became an orderly, efficient community with a European atmosphere.

▼ Nahariya Beach   Crusaders fort, Judin ▶

Acre (Akko)

A sea port from ancient times, Acre lay on the Via Maris and had connections with the cross-country highway to the east, and the Way of the Patriarchs linking Egypt to the empires of the north. It was first mentioned 4000 years ago in the Egyptian Execration Texts, and later in the Amarna letters and other documents of the fifteenth-thirteenth centuries B.C.

When Joshua entered Canaan and divided it up among the Children of Israel, Acre and

Lookout point on the old city wall ▲

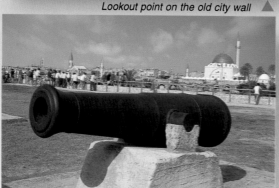

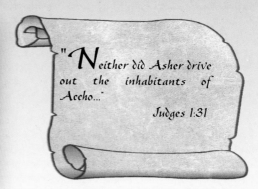

"*Neither did Asher drive out the inhabitants of Accho...*"

Judges 1:31

Ancient Turkish Cannon ▲

its surroundings fell to the lot of Asher.

Acre opened its gates to Alexander the Great and was rewarded by permission to be virtually independent and to mint its own coins. Renamed Ptolemais, it continued to thrive, although neither the Hasmoneans nor the Herodians managed to annex it to their kingdoms. Under the Romans it became the army headquarters, and from here assaults were launched on the Jewish strongholds of the Galilee. The Muslims took the town in 636 and reverted to the use of its ancient name.

In 1104 the Crusaders finally took Acre and made it their capital, setting up the Kingdom of Acre which lasted until 1291. They renamed it St Jean d'Acre and it was ruled by the Knights of St John. During this period, Acre's wealth and economic output were legendary. The wonderfully preserved, now subterranean, Crusaders' city with its enormous complex of knights' halls with vaulted ceilings and stone floors bear witness to its greatness. These halls were used as living quarters, dining halls, a hospice and for ceremonial purposes. For centuries they were choked with debris up to the springers

Khan el Umdan with clock tower ▲

▼ *Aerial view of Old Acre with the city wall and moat in the foreground*

Interior of the Municipal Museum ▲

of the arches. Today the enormous knights' hall is often used for concerts. Through the vast and impressive administrative halls is the Crypt of St John, which once served as the Knight Hospitalers' dining hall. Its vaulted ceiling is supported by three colossal round pillars. A secret underground tunnel once led from here to the harbor to enable the knights to flee in case of siege.

The city was taken by the Mamelukes in 1291 and only began to pick up in the seventeeth century.

In 1781, Ahmed el-Jazzar, known as the Butcher for his extreme cruelty, erected

▼St John's Crypt.   ▲Interior of the Mosque

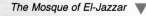
The Mosque of El-Jazzar ▼

the Great Mosque, with marble columns shipped in from Ashkelon and Caesarea. It is built in Turkish style over the foundations of the Crusader cathedral, and Ahmed el-Jazzar and his adopted son and successor, Suleiman, are both buried here. The mosque has a shrine containing a single hair from the beard of the prophet Mohammed but the rest of the interior is impressive for its starkness. In front of the mosque is a charming garden with a lovely fountain. El-Jazzar also built the Hammam - the Baths - now the Municipal Museum, the Khan el-Umdan (of the Pillars) - and the aqueduct bringing water from the springs of Kabri. With the help of the British, El-Jazzar staved off Napoleon's two-month siege of Acre in 1799. Later, with the advent of steamships, the port lost its importance and the city sank into obscurity.

The old city within the walls is famous for its fishing harbor, souk and its narrow, picturesque lanes.

The Citadel, built by El-Jazzar on Crusader ruins, was used for military purposes and later became a prison, which was most recently used during the British Mandate when many Jewish fighters were incarcerated and executed here.

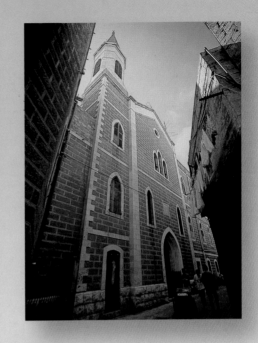

▲ *Seaside promenade with light-house*

▼ *The marina*

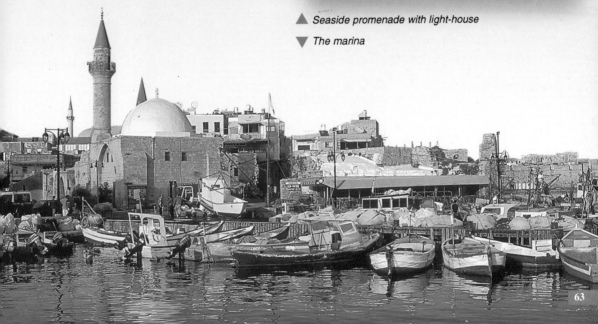

The Bahai Shrine, the terraced gardens ▲

The seat of the Bahai Universal House of Justice ▲

Haifa

aifa is a modern harbor able to accommodate all sorts of luxury liners, tankers, cargo boats and other ships. Along the quays are grain silos, warehouses, a container terminal, repair shops and all the facilities needed for equipping every kind of vessel. Giant vats mark the Haifa refineries, once the terminal of the Iraqi oil pipeline and now utilized for Israel's own requirements. Wide, shady roads climb the hills behind the town to attractive suburbs where building is going on apace, and the Technion and Haifa University are turning out highly-qualified engineers and scholars in every field. Today Haifa is Israel's Silicon Valley, with many internationally known companies specializing in high technology.

Haifa's landscape from the sea is dominated by the golden dome of the Bahai Temple. Set in formal gardens is the grave of the Persian-born Bab - the Gate, or the Forerunner - who was executed in 1850 at the age of 31 for his religious teachings.

Haifa by night ▼

Ideally situated as it is, between the sea and forested Mount Carmel, the environs of Haifa have been a favorite habitation for untold generations. Prehistoric man lived here in the caves of Mount Carmel. Before the coming of the Israelites, there were Phoenicians at Shikmona on the coast directly south of Haifa and to the north-west, near the present suburb of Bat Galim. Phoenician fishermen produced the famous Royal Purple dye

from the murex snails found locally and, it is said, introduced the craft of glass-making with the fine silica sand on the shore.

During the Talmudic period, Haifa was overwhelmingly Jewish, famed for its scholars, sailors and craftsmen. Together with the Arabs who had come in with the invasion of 636, the Jews unsuccessfully tried to resist the Crusader troops. Wrested from the Crusaders and destroyed by the Mamelukes in 1265, Haifa remained an insignificant colony for 500 years until after World War 1 when the British made full use of the port, and since then it has never looked back.

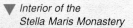

▲ Stella Maris Monastery

Haifa has a number of outstanding museums including the Maritime Museum, the Museum of Ethnology, the Dagon Grain Museum, a Japanese Art Museum and the National Museum of Science and Technology.

▼ Interior of the Stella Maris Monastery

Stella Maris

At the top of the promontory, with a magnificent view of the city of Haifa, is the largest Carmelite Monastery and world center of the Order, built on the site of earlier

▼ Stella Maris Monastery, Grotto of Saint Elias

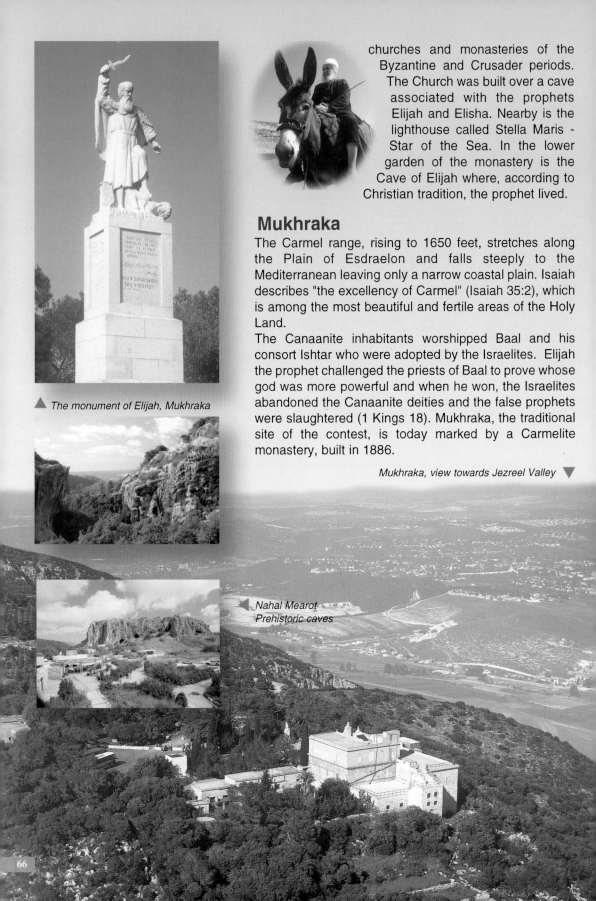

churches and monasteries of the Byzantine and Crusader periods. The Church was built over a cave associated with the prophets Elijah and Elisha. Nearby is the lighthouse called Stella Maris - Star of the Sea. In the lower garden of the monastery is the Cave of Elijah where, according to Christian tradition, the prophet lived.

Mukhraka

The Carmel range, rising to 1650 feet, stretches along the Plain of Esdraelon and falls steeply to the Mediterranean leaving only a narrow coastal plain. Isaiah describes "the excellency of Carmel" (Isaiah 35:2), which is among the most beautiful and fertile areas of the Holy Land.

The Canaanite inhabitants worshipped Baal and his consort Ishtar who were adopted by the Israelites. Elijah the prophet challenged the priests of Baal to prove whose god was more powerful and when he won, the Israelites abandoned the Canaanite deities and the false prophets were slaughtered (1 Kings 18). Mukhraka, the traditional site of the contest, is today marked by a Carmelite monastery, built in 1886.

The monument of Elijah, Mukhraka

Mukhraka, view towards Jezreel Valley ▼

Nahal Mearot Prehistoric caves

▲ *The mosque is the only remnant of the village founded by Serbian Muslims in 1809*

Above right: Stone with an inscription mentioning Pontius Pilate ◀

▼ *Remains of the Roman harbor*

Caesarea

Against the glittering background of the sea rises the restored Crusader city of Caesarea, with its moat and battlements, its vaulted halls, churches, flag-stoned streets, cisterns and dwellings. This was but one chapter in the long annals of Caesarea, constructed by Herod in 20 B.C on the site of the Phoenician anchorage of Straton's Tower, and named for Augustus Caesar. Josephus tells in his Antiquities (book 15:9), that Herod "erected edifices of white stone and sumptuous palaces...also a theater of stone and, on the south, an amphitheater." The Roman theater, cleared and renovated, is now used in the summer for concerts and other performances. An elaborate water-supply system brought water from the Carmel range via an aqueduct: the Romans

▼ *Remains of the Crusader tower in the harbor.*

Roman porphyry and marble statues
re-erected in the Byzantine street

Part of
a newly excavated mosaic

needed large quantities of water for their baths and fountains as well as for irrigation. Herod also built a silt-free deep-water harbor, an amazing engineering feat for its time, with storehouses and offices.

For 600 years, Caesarea was the capital of the Roman province of Judea and official residence of its governors, including Pontius Pilate. Simon Peter preached to a gentile congregation here at the house of Cornelius the Centurion, the first pagan to be baptized a Christian (Acts 10). From here, Paul was sent on his missions abroad and Acts 9:30 relates how he was "brought down to Caesarea and sent to Tarsus". He was imprisoned in

East
Gate

Herod's
Amphitheater

Roman
Theater

Promontory
Palace

Cardo
Maximus

Caesarea and then, when "King Agrippa and Bernice came unto Caesarea" (Acts 25:13) he talked with them. Here in 66 A.D. began the Jewish revolt against the Romans when 20,000 Jews were killed by pagans in a pogrom. Vespasian was crowned emperor in Caesarea in 70 and granted it the status of a colony. At the end of the Bar Kochba rebellion in 135, the great Jewish scholar Rabbi Akiba was tortured and killed here by the Romans. Christianity quickly gained ground in Caesarea and the Christian scholars Origen and Eusebius lived here in the third and fourth centuries. It was the seat of a bishop during the Byzantine period and the remains of the Byzantine street lined with shops can still be seen. After a bitter struggle, Caesarea fell to the Persians in 646 but they kept it well. "Its milk and white bread are famous", wrote a tenth century geographer about Caesarea, "and its fruit delicious." Under the Crusaders it was built as a citadel-town of some 50 acres, less than a tenth of the Herodian city. They built many impressive buildings, including a cathedral, often using stones, marble pillars and other remains of Roman and Byzantine buildings. The massive fortified walls and moat of this period, built under the French king Louis IX, still surround the city. It prospered until it was conquered by the Mameluke sultan Beybars in 1291, and was virtually abandoned.

▲ *The Roman theater*

▲ *The entrance gate*

The high level aqueduct ▼

▲ *The Crusader city wall and moat*

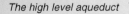

Megiddo
Armageddon

Megiddo's strategic location overlooking the Plain of Jezreel and dominating the trade routes from Egypt to Mesopotamia has made it a site of extreme importance since time immemorial.

The tel of Megiddo consists of twenty superimposed cities, the oldest dating back to 4000 B.C. There was a Canaanite city here around 2000 B.C which was fortified in the 18th century by the Hyksos and then conquered by Pharoah Thutmose of Egypt in 1478 B.C. This fact was recorded in ancient Egyptian texts and was considered to be a great victory. Megiddo was one of the walled city-states taken by Joshua. Rich and powerful under the united monarchy, I Kings 9 recalls how Solomon raised a levy to build "the wall of Jerusalem and Hazor, and Megiddo, and Gezer". After he had fortified it, he made it one of his chariot cities. Pharoah Shishak of Egypt occupied the city in 915 B.C. after taking away the treasures of the temple of Jerusalem. The next conquerors were

Above: The lion seal found in Megiddo with the Hebrew inscription "belonging to Shema, servant of Jerusalem"

Bird's eye view of the ancient tel of Megiddo

"The spirits of the devils working miracles, which go forth unto the kings of the earth and of the whole world, to gather them to the battle of that great day of God Almighty... And he gathered them together into a place called in Hebrew tongue Armegeddon".

Revelation 16:14-16

Canaanite altar at Megiddo

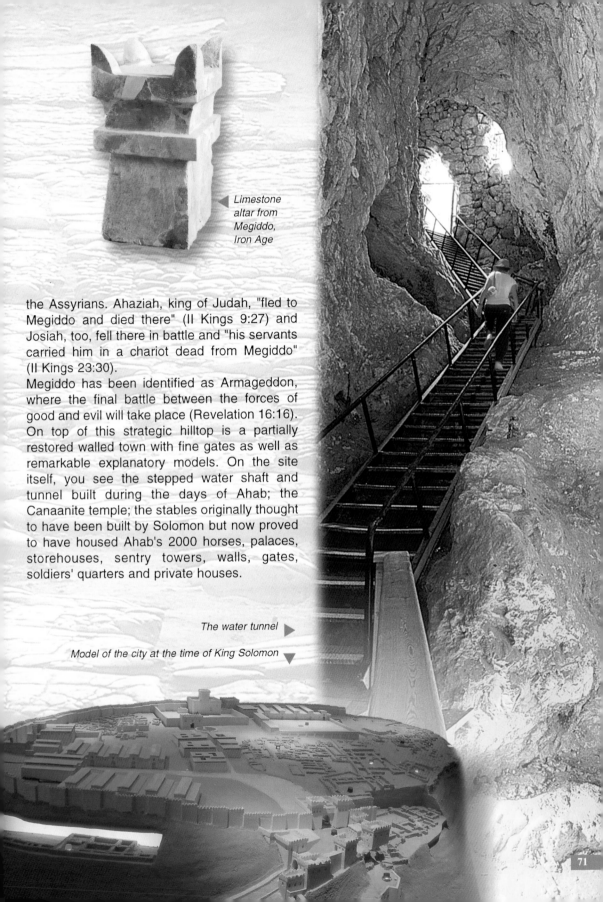

Limestone altar from Megiddo, Iron Age

the Assyrians. Ahaziah, king of Judah, "fled to Megiddo and died there" (II Kings 9:27) and Josiah, too, fell there in battle and "his servants carried him in a chariot dead from Megiddo" (II Kings 23:30).

Megiddo has been identified as Armageddon, where the final battle between the forces of good and evil will take place (Revelation 16:16). On top of this strategic hilltop is a partially restored walled town with fine gates as well as remarkable explanatory models. On the site itself, you see the stepped water shaft and tunnel built during the days of Ahab; the Canaanite temple; the stables originally thought to have been built by Solomon but now proved to have housed Ahab's 2000 horses, palaces, storehouses, sentry towers, walls, gates, soldiers' quarters and private houses.

The water tunnel ▶

Model of the city at the time of King Solomon ▼

71

Jezreel Valley
(Esdraelon)

Bet Shearim, the burial cave

In antiquity, as today, the Jezreel Valley was crossed by major arterial roads. The Valley extends from Bet Shearim in the west to the valley of Bet Shean in the east and to Jenin in the south. The Via Maris, linking Egypt with Mesapotamia, was the primary route along which armies and caravans could pass from the coastal plain into the Jordan Valley and the Jezreel Valley was therefore of utmost strategic importance. Throughout the ages, many battles for its domination have taken place. The Canaanites, who had superior chariots, forced the Israelites to take to the mountains (Josh. 17:16). In the time of the Judges, the armies of Gideon and Deborah fought here, turning their command of the surrounding highlands against their well-armed enemies.

In more recent times, Napoleon fought here in 1799 and the British General Allenby in 1917.

Jezreel Valley and Mount Tabor

The Jezreel valley was known for its fertile land from ancient times and today is still considered Israel's bread-basket. Due to neglect over the years, the entire area became a malarial swamp until the land was reclaimed by Jewish settlers and transformed into fertile farmland. In the valley was the ancient city of Jezreel where Naboth had his vineyard "hard by the palace of Ahab king of Samaria" (I Kings 21:1), and where Jezebel was killed by Jehu (II Kings 9:33).

(well of) Harod where Gideon, in his fight against the Midianites, "pitched beside the well of Harod". By these same waters, Gideon, at the Lord's command, tested the men who were to accompany him to war. "The number of them that lapped, putting their hand to their mouth, were three hundred" (Judges 7). Nearby is the Sakhne, or Gan Hashlosha, with rockpools, waterfalls and ancient water-mills, today a National Park, and an idyllic site for picnics.

Mount Gilboa

At the foot of Mount Gilboa, I Samuel 31:8 describes how..."they found Saul and his three sons fallen" in battle with the Philistines. In his lament over Saul and Jonathon, his beloved friend, David cries out and curses the spot: "The beauty of Israel is slain upon thy high places: how are the mighty fallen...Ye mountains of Gilboa, let there be no dew, neither let there be rain" (II Sam 1:19). Despite the curse, there are flourishing trees and wild flowers on its slopes, and at the foot of the mountain are springs and pools steeped in lush vegetation. One of these well-watered spots is Ein

Mount Gilboa ▲

Mount Gilboa, bird's eye view from the east ▼

Bet Shean

"Tyche", fragment of the mosaic floor of a Byzantine public building

Bet Shean, the Greek Scythopolis, was one of the great cities of olden days. An important junction from which roads fanned out north to Syria, east to Jordan, south to Egypt and west to the Mediterranean, it was at all times a supply center for the varied produce growing in the area. Excavations show 18 levels of occupation, from the Chalcolithic era (the fourth millennium B.C.) onward. Finds included Egyptian temples and several stelae inscribed with hieroglyphic writing. These and other items discovered prove that for at least three hundred years, from about the fifteenth to the twelfth centuries B.C., Bet Shean was the administrative headquarters of Egyptian rule. Allotted to the tribe of Manasseh, there were difficulties with the local population and Joshua 17:12 states that the children of Manasseh could not drive out the inhabitants, although apparently they lived peaceably with the Canaanites.

The excavations

I Samuel 31:10 tells of Saul's death in battle with the Philistines, who "fastened his body to the walls of Beth-shean". During the time of Christ, the city was one of the Graeco-Roman cities of the Decapolis, an alliance of cities on both sides of the Jordan. From the Hasmonean era many Jews lived in the city. They were massacred around 70 A.D., at the end of the Roman-Jewish war, but in the Talmudic period Jews resettled there and were active in learning and commerce. Flax was grown, linen woven and cloth manufactured, for Bet Shean was then a world center for the textile trade and for food production. Jew and Gentile seem to have coexisted side by side, for in addition to the Roman theater dating from 200 A.D., remains of several large synagogues were found, including one with a Samaritan inscription. There are also remains of a Roman colonnaded street which was once lined with shops.

The early Arab period saw the continuation of Bet Shean's prosperity, and it was famed for its dates, rice and vineyards. However in 749 an earthquake felled the town and thereafter it fell into obscurity.

The Roman theater ▲

▲ *Bet Shean, bird's eye view*

Judea & Samaria

Apollonia

Nablus

Sebastia

Jacob's Well

Samaria

Mt Gerizim

Antipatris

Judea

Shiloh

Bethel

Jaffa

Jerusalem

Mt of Olives

Lod

Ramla

Emmaus

Jericho

Ein Karem

Bethany

Qumran

Bethlehem

Valley of Elah

Herodium

Mar Saba

Beth Guvrin

Dead Sea

Ein Gedi

Hebron

Masada

Arad

Ein karem

Ein Karem is the village "in the hill country of Judah" (Luke 1:65) where John the Baptist was born. Here Zacharias, John the Baptist's father, had his summer home, and here the Virgin Mary visited her cousin Elisabeth. Churches, convents and monasteries abound in the picturesque valley, while around Mary's Spring, from which Mary is said to have drawn water when she visited her cousin Elisabeth, there are artists' galleries and a popular Music Center.

▲ *The Church of the Visitation*

Above right: Sanctuary of the Visitation - The Magnificat

▼ *Interior of the Church of the Visitation*

The Baptism
of Jesus
by St. John,
Ein Karem

The oldest churches are those of St. John the Baptist and Visitation, both belonging to the Franciscans. The Church of St. John the Baptist is built over the birthplace of St. John and has beautiful paintings and decorated ceramic tiles. The first church on the site was erected in Byzantine times and rebuilt by the Crusaders, but later destroyed. The present structure was completed in 1674. Steps lead down to a natural cave, the Grotto of the Birth of St. John. A verse from the "Benedictus" is inscribed on the lintel: "Blessed be the Lord, God of Israel; for he hath visited and redeemed his people".

The two-story Church of the Visitation, designed by Barluzzi, was completed in 1955. A chapel built on the site of the home of Elizabeth and Zacharias has paintings describing events in their lives. Behind a grill is the rock where the baby John is said to have been concealed during the Massacre of the Innocents. The courtyard is decorated with ceramic tiles bearing the "Magnificat" in 42 languages.

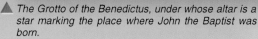

The Grotto of the Benedictus, under whose altar is a star marking the place where John the Baptist was born.

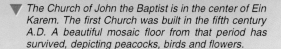

The Church of John the Baptist is in the center of Ein Karem. The first Church was built in the fifth century A.D. A beautiful mosaic floor from that period has survived, depicting peacocks, birds and flowers.

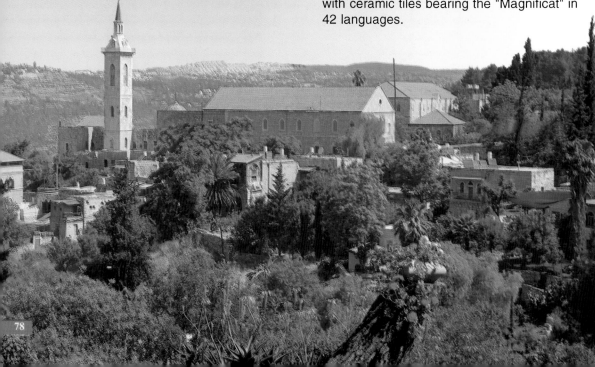

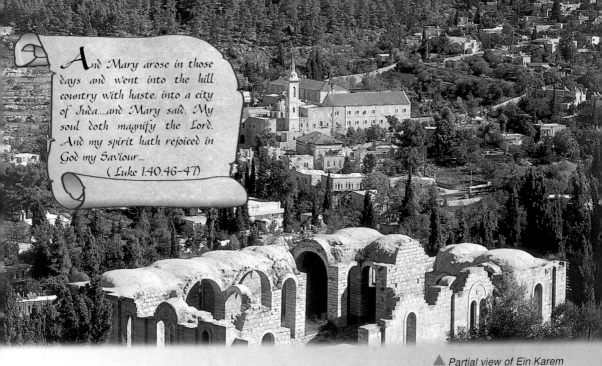

And Mary arose in those days and went into the hill country with haste, into a city of Juda....and Mary said, My soul doth magnify the Lord. And my spirit hath rejoiced in God my Saviour...
(Luke 1:40,46–47)

▲ *Partial view of Ein Karem*

Kathisma

A rock known as Kathisma, Greek for "the seat", at the center of a large octagonal fifth century Byzantine church, is said to be the rock on which Mary stopped to rest on her way from Jerusalem to Bethlehem before giving birth to Jesus.
The site is owned by the Greek Orthodox Church.

▼ *Kathisma, on the road between Jerusalem and Bethlehem*

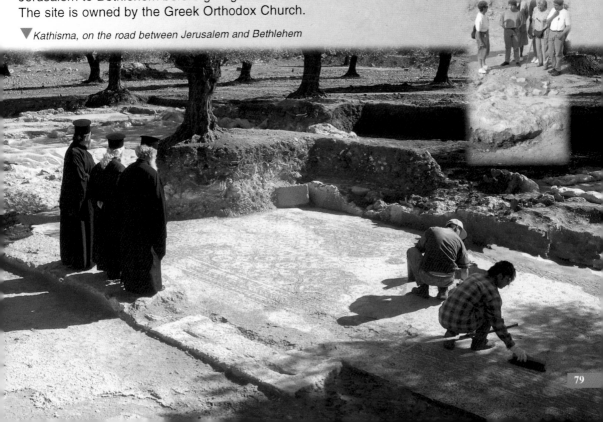

"And Joseph also went up....unto the city of David, which is called Bethlehem..To be taxed with Mary his espoused wife, being great with child....And she brought forth her firstborn son, and wrapped him in swaddling clothes, and laid him in a manger: because there was no room for them in the inn.

Luke 2:4-7

Bethlehem

The little town of Bethlehem, which in Hebrew means "house of bread", has many biblical associations reflecting a tranquil, pastoral existence. As its name signifies, in antiquity the district was known for its fertility and for the cultivation of its fields and terraces. In the Old Testament, Bethlehem is often referred to as Ephrat, which means fruitfulness. Here, nearly four thousand years ago, Jacob buried his young wife Rachel; here was the home of Naomi and her family; here Ruth gleaned in the fields and fell in love with her kinsman Boaz; here their great-grandson David was born and here Samuel "anointed him in the midst of his brethren" (1 Samuel 16:13).

But the event which took place here and transformed the course of history was that "Jesus was born in Bethlehem of Judea" (Matthew 2:1) Today, this town, surrounded by a beautiful hilly landscape, is the home of Christian and Muslim Arabs, many of whom are skilled artisans and craftsmen.

The Church
of St. Catherine

The Church of the Nativity

Herodium

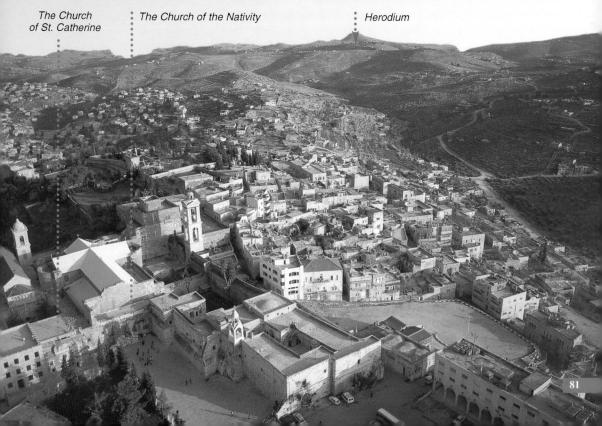

Church of the Nativity

Detail of a column
in the Basilica of the Nativity

Luke 2:7 describes how Mary "brought forth her firstborn son...and laid him in a manger; because there was not room in the inn". Over this cave-like manger, traditionally Jesus' birthplace, arose the Basilica of the Nativity.

From the very beginnings of the Christian era this was a sacred grotto, above which, in the fourth century, Emperor Constantine constructed a large church, first piercing a hole in the cave roof for the faithful to look down into the holy place, then erecting an octagonal altar over it. The altar is still there. Around two hundred years later, Emperor Justinian rebuilt the basilica much as it is seen today, and put up a mosaic pediment of the Magi in Persian dress. Because of this picture, it is claimed, the ravaging Persian troops of 614 spared the Church of the Nativity from destruction. No basic changes were made by the Crusaders, except for the decoration of the church with rich paintings and glass mosaics.

The entrance to the Basilica of the Nativity, which is shared by the Armenians, the Greek Orthodox and the Latins, has been filled in below the straight wide Byzantine lintel to outline the pointed Crusader doorway. This in turn was partially blocked by the Turks, leaving the present opening

Basilica of the Nativity

Church of the Nativity with
the Church of St. Catherine on the left

small to allow for easy defence and to prevent horses and other animals from entering the Church. The rectangular prayer hall is approximately 200 by 90 feet, with four rows of twelve brown Bethlehem stone pillars. The oak ceiling was donated by Edward IV of England and Duke Philip of Burgundy in 1482. There is a pink marble font to the right and the original eight-sided altar directly ahead. In the floor are trapdoors through which remains of the mosaic floor of the original church can be seen.

Curved steps descend to the Grotto, where a silver star overlies the spot of Jesus' birth. It bears the Latin inscription "Hic de virgine Maria Jesus Christus natus est - 1717" - here Jesus Christ was born of the Virgin Mary - 1717. Nearby, in the Chapel of the Manger, which belongs to the Greek Orthodox, Mary is said to have laid the Child.

" *And* Joseph also went up....unto the city of David. which is called Bethlehem.. To be taxed with Mary his espoused wife. being great with child....And she brought forth her firstborn son. and wrapped him in swaddling clothes. and laid him in a manger: because there was no room for them in the inn.

Luke 2:4-7

▲ *Crusader bishop's staff from the twelfth century*

▲ *The Star of Bethlehem*

▼ *The Grotto of the Nativity*

Chapel of St Catherine

Adjacent to the Church of the Nativity is the Franciscan Chapel of St. Catherine of Alexandria, sensitively restored by Antonio Barluzzi in 1933. From here, Bethlehem's annual midnight mass on Christmas is broadcast all over the world. A statue of St. Jerome, who lived here in the fifth century and translated the Bible into Latin, stands in the middle of the courtyard. Interesting crypts, said to be the burial places of St. Jerome, St. Paula and St. Eusebius of Cremona, honeycomb the rock. Another door, always kept locked, links the crypt with the Grotto of the Nativity. Within the Church of St. Catherine are the Chapel of St. Joseph where Joseph was commanded by an angel to flee to Egypt, and the Chapel of the Innocents, commemorating the massacre of the babies killed by Herod.

December 24, the Christmas procession in Manger Square

Arabs riding their camels in the vicinity of Bethlehem, reminiscent of the "Three Wise Men"

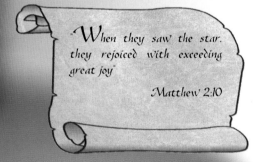

"When they saw the star, they rejoiced with exceeding great joy"

Matthew 2:10

*The Church
of St. Catherine
on Christmas Eve* ▶

Christmas Eve
in Bethlehem

The focus of Christmas celebrations in Bethlehem is Manger Square, just outside the Basilica of the Nativity. Christmas is observed on different dates by different denominations - the western Christians celebrate on the night of 24th December, the Greek Orthodox on 7th January and the Armenians on 19th January. Each is celebrated by colorful processions led by the Patriarch of its sect. On the western Christmas, choirs from all over the world sing together in the square and the mass, which is celebrated in St. Catherine's church, is broadcast to over fifty countries. Those unable to get into the church can watch the service on a giant screen in the square.

*The Patriarch carries
the Child
of Bethlehem.* ▶

*The Church
of the Nativity
on Christmas Eve*
▼

Shepherds' Field

Fresco depicting the angel announcing the birth of Jesus to the shepherds.

Shepherds still pasture their flocks around Bethlehem, where the shepherds heard the good tidings of Jesus' birth from the angel of the Lord who told them to go to Bethlehem to adore the child (Luke 2). "Shepherds' Field", sometimes called Ruth's field, is near the village of Bet Sahur. Everywhere, evidence is found of Byzantine convents, and a Greek Orthodox church covers a cave which has a fine fourth century mosaic floor. Another church, called "Campo Dei Pastori" - "Shepherd's Field" was rebuilt for the Franciscans by Antonio Barluzzi in 1950. The design of the Church represents a shepherd's tent and the light penetrating the church through the glass openings of the dome recall the light that shone on the shepherds when the angel appeared to give them the tidings of Jesus' birth. The walls are decorated with frescoes depicting the story of the shepherds and in the center of the Church is an altar supported by bronze statues of shepherds.

The Shepherds' Field Church

"And there were in the same country shepherds abiding in the fields, keeping watch over their flock by night. And so, the angel of the Lord shone round about them... And the angel said unto them, fear not: for, behold, I bring you good tidings of great joy, which shall be to all people. For unto you is born this day in the City of David a Saviour, which is Christ the Lord... And it came to pass as the angels were gone away from them into heaven, the shepherds said one to another "Let us now go even unto Bethlehem and see this thing which is come to pass"

(Luke 2:8-15).

▲ Interior of the Shepherds' Field Church

▼ Sheep grazing near Bethlehem

"And a certain man of Beth-Lehem judah went to sojourn in the country of Moab, he and his wife, and his two sons.

Ruth 1:1

87

The Entrance to the Franciscan church which was built in 1871 over the Milk Grotto.

Church of the Milk Grotto

The milky white Church of the Milk Grotto is a Franciscan chapel built over the cave in which the Holy Family sheltered during the flight to Egypt. When King Herod heard from the three wise men that the new-born king of the Jews had been born in Bethlehem, he ordered all male children aged two years and less to

The interior of the Milk Grotto which commemorates the Christian doctrine of the Divine Maternity of the Virgin Mary.

> "**A**nd when they were departed, behold, the angel of the Lord appeared to Joseph in a dream, saying, Arise, and take the young Child and his mother, and flee into Egypt, and bide thou there until I bring thee word: for Herod will seek the young child to destroy him.' When he arose, he took the young child and his mother by night, and departed into Egypt, and was there until the death of Herod."
>
> Matthew 2:13–14

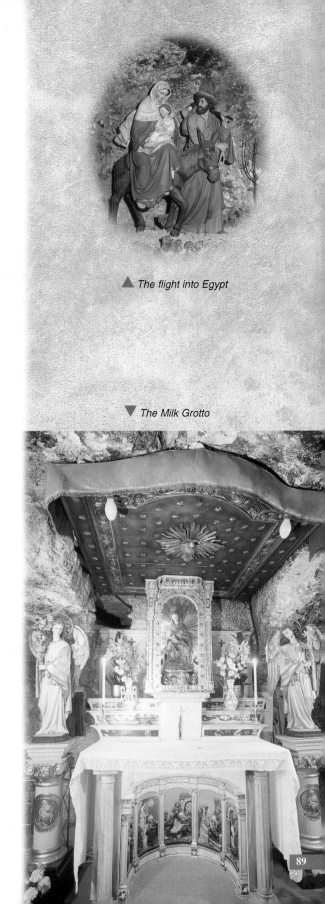

▲ The flight into Egypt

▼ The Milk Grotto

be killed. An angel warned the Holy Family of these murders, and they fled to Egypt. Tradition holds that while nursing the baby, some of Mary's milk spilled on the stone floor, turning the entire cave white. Packets of the powdered white stone are sold there and are especially popular with nursing mothers who believe that the powder will ensure a plentiful supply of milk.

From the Milk Grotto in Bethlehem
(Contemporary Palestinian Art)

The Market

On weekday mornings, Manger Square is alive with a typical Oriental market, attended by women from the surrounding villages wearing the traditional colorful local dress. Here one can find everything from sweet Arab cakes dripping in honey to statuettes and other artifacts carved in olive wood. Mother-of-pearl religious objects are also made here; in the late sixteenth century, the custodian of Bethlehem encouraged the poverty-stricken inhabitants to make these souvenirs for sale to pilgrims. To this day, most Bethlehemites live off tourism and there are many souvenir shops around the square.

At the market in Bethlehem

▼ *"Bethlehem" in Hebrew is "House of Bread"*

▼ *"Bethlehem" in Arabic is "House of Meat"*

Rachel's Tomb

Rachel's Tomb is a small domed structure marking the grave of Jacob's favorite wife, who died giving birth to Benjamin and "was buried on the way to Ephrath, which is Bethlehem" (Gen. 35:19). Revered by Christians and Muslims as well as Jews, the tomb is - and has been for generations - a place of Jewish pilgrimage, where throngs of people, particularly childless wives, come to pray to the youngest and loveliest of the Matriarchs.

Mentioned as early as 333 by the Bordeaux Pilgrim as being "covered by a pyramid of stones", it was rebuilt by the Crusaders who protected the cenotaph by a domed roof supported on four columns. In 1788, the arches were blocked to form a closed chamber. In 1841 Sir Moses Montefiore repaired the building and added a vestibule with a mihrab, or south-pointing prayer niche, for Muslim worship.

▲ *The Tomb of Rachel*

Herodion

Set on a high hilltop in the Judean wilderness is the strange, truncated cone of Herodion, built by Herod the Great in 37 B.C. and described in detail by Josephus Flavius in his "Wars of the Jews". Archaeological digs have confirmed that in this remarkable construction Herod "built round towers all about the top, and filled the remaining space with costly palaces...He brought a mighty quantity of water from a great distance, and raised an ascent of two hundred marble steps of the whitest marble." Within the enclosure are remnants of Herod's fresco-painted halls and chambers, a bath-house and one of the earliest underground synagogues ever discovered. Herod, Josephus writes, died in Jericho in 4 A.D, and was placed on "a bier of all gold, embroidered with precious stones...and a crown of gold on his head...and the body was carried to Herodion". His grave has not yet been found.

▼ *The hill of Herodion*

St. Mary of the Hortus Conclusus

▲ St Mary of the Hortus Conclusus

Close to Solomon's Pools is a convent which was built in the nineteenth century by an Argentinian bishop. The small fertile valley in which it is situated is said to be the enclosed garden, the hortus conclusus of the Song of Solomon 4:12: "A garden inclosed is my sister, my spouse".

Kalat el-Burak
The Castle of the Pools

The Castle of the Pools was built in Turkish times to guard the triple reservoirs called "Solomon's Pools", so-called from Solomon's declaration in Ecclesiastes 2:6 "I made me pools of water". Partly rock-hewn, partly masonry-built and plaster-lined, these enormous artificial pools filled with rainwater which collected from the surrounding hills to feed Herod's elaborate system of aqueducts supplying Jerusalem with water at all seasons.

▲ Sheep grazing near Bethlehem

"I made me pools of water to irrigate a grove of growing trees."
Ecclesiastes 2:6

▼ Solomon's Pools

Hebron

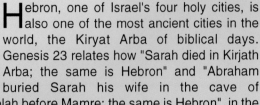

Ruins of ancient Mamre ▲

Hebron, one of Israel's four holy cities, is also one of the most ancient cities in the world, the Kiryat Arba of biblical days. Genesis 23 relates how "Sarah died in Kirjath Arba; the same is Hebron" and "Abraham buried Sarah his wife in the cave of Machpelah before Mamre: the same is Hebron", in the field which he bought from Ephron the Hittite for "four hundred shekels of silver". Abraham himself was later buried here, as were Isaac and Rebecca, and Jacob and Leah. Legend holds that the graves of Adam and Eve were also in the same place.

For seven years David reigned in Hebron as king of Judah. Almost a thousand years later Herod the Great erected the wall encircling the compound. In Byzantine times it was roofed over and turned into the Church of St. Abraham. With the Moslem invasion of 636, the Church became the Mosque of Abraham and except for the interval of Crusader domination, from 1099 to 1187, it has remained so ever since. The Tomb of the Patriarchs has always been one of Jewry's most hallowed shrines, though for centuries Jews were forbidden to ascend beyond the seventh step of the entrance staircase. Now, all pilgrims may, at specified times, enter the prayer halls with the symbolic cenotaphs set over the graves in the cave-mausoleum of the Patriarchs.

Symbolic cenotaphs set over ▲
the graves - mausoleum
of the Patriarchs and Matriarchs.

"*There, they buried Abraham and Sarah his wife: there they buried Isaac and Rebecca his wife: and there I buried Leah.*

Genesis 49:31

▼ *The Cave*
of Machpelah

Samaria

Samaritans waving the Torah Scrolls on Mount Gerizim

Many villages in the historic hill-country of Samaria are mentioned in the Bible. Sebastia, the Roman name for the ancient city of Samaria, was founded in 876 B.C by Omri as capital of the northern kingdom of Israel which, after the death of Solomon, had broken away from Judah. His son Ahab, husband of Jezebel, embellished the city, which became a center of idol-worship and corruption, incurring the wrath of the prophet Elijah. In 722 B.C it was destroyed by the Assyrians and its inhabitants, who became the Ten Lost Tribes, were exiled. It was rebuilt by Alexander the Great and during the Herodian and Roman periods, Sebastia was a flourishing city, with columned streets, a forum, theater and hippodrome, protected by a wall with gates.

Mount Gerizim and Mount Ebal stand like sentries on either side of Nablus and of its predecessor, Shechem. These two mountains appear very early in Bible chronology, for as soon as Joshua entered the Promised Land, he "built an altar unto the Lord God of Israel in Mount Ebal...and wrote there upon the stones a copy of the law of Moses" (Joshua 8:30-33).

▲ Samaritans on their way to the ceremony of Waving the Torah Scroll, held during the Festival of Pentecost.

"And it shall come to pass when the Lord thy God hath brought thee in unto the land whither thou goest to possess it, that thou shalt put the blessing upon mount Gerizim, and the curse upon mount Ebal.
Deut. 11:29

▼ Excavations on Mount Gerizim

Jacob's Well ▼

The Samaritans

The Samaritans, who at the dawn of the Christian era were counted in their hundreds of thousands, today number around 500. They claim descent from Ephraim and Manasseh, sons of Joseph. They accept only the Pentateuch as the Holy Writ and all its precepts are meticulously honored. Mount Gerizim, rather than Mount Moriah, is considered the holy mountain and is the focus of the three pilgrim festivals of the Samaritans. On their Passover festival, they re-enact the biblical scenes of the slaughter and roasting of the pascal lambs, with each man obeying the order that "ye shall eat it with your loins girded, your shoes on your feet and your staff in your hand" (Exodus 12:11). The Samaritans' Temple on Mount Gerizim rivaled that of Jerusalem until it was destroyed by the Hasmonean ruler, John Hyrcanus, in 128 B.C. The Roman emperor Hadrian built a pagan temple to Jupiter above its ruins, and over that arose two Byzantine churches.

Jacob's Well

On the border of Mount Gerizim, in the village of Askar, biblical Sychar, is the Well of Jacob, dug by the Patriarch over 3000 years ago. John 4:5-6 tells the story of how Jesus came "to a city of Samaria, which is called Sychar...now Jacob's well was there" and here, "being wearied with his journey, sat thus on the well.." and met the woman of Samaria. Considered a holy spot from early in the fourth century, when a church was put up over the well, it has remained a place of pilgrimage ever since.

*Ruins
of the
Roman forum*

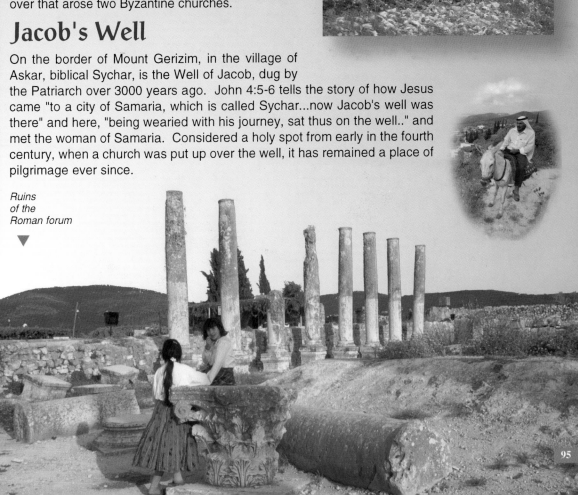

Life in the time of Jesus

Winnowing

Drawing water from well

Writing scrolls

Weaver

Photographed in the Hasmonean village, near Modiin.

Street scenes

Milestone marked "Jericho world's oldest city", on the road to Jericho.

Jericho

The new mosque

Jericho - the City of Palms - one of the oldest cities in the world, lies 800 feet below sea-level in a plain traversed by the River Jordan. At Tel es-Sultan are remains of an 8000 B.C settlement. In 3000 B.C., Jericho was an important Canaanite town which, after being encircled by Joshua, fell to the blast of the priests' trumpets in about 1250 B.C, the first city to be taken by the Israelites. Although Joshua had forbidden the rebuilding of the city, in the ninth century B.C "Hiel the Bethelite did build Jericho" (1 Kings 16:34). Joshua's curse came true, for Hiel lost, or perhaps sacrificed, his oldest son Abiram and his youngest son Segub. Despite

A shop in Jericho, the "city of palms", where locally grown dates, bananas and early-ripening oranges are offered for sale

The town center

The Spring
of Elisha
(Ain es Sultan)

the curse, the city lasted four hundred years. Opposite the tel is the Spring of Elisha, or Sultan's Spring, where the prophet healed the spring of water by throwing salt in it (II Kings 2). In the first century B.C. Mark Anthony presented the city to Cleopatra, who leased it to Herod. He enlarged it and built a winter palace some distance from the ancient town, on higher land

The sycomore
tree of Jericho

"And Jesus entered and passed through Jericho. And behold, there was a man named Zacchaeus, which was the chief among the publicans... and he sought to see Jesus who he was... and he ran before, and climbed up into a sycomore tree to see him: for he was to pass that way..."

Luke 19:5-9

Partial view
of Jericho

Excavations at the ancient Tel es Sultan with the Mt. of Temptation in the background.

overlooking the Dead Sea. It was in the swimming pool of this palace that he drowned his popular brother-in-law. This was New Testament Jericho, through which Jesus passed on his way to Jerusalem, about two miles south of the biblical city. The sycomore fig, the tree which Zacchaeus climbed in order to catch a glimpse of Jesus, still grows in the area.

The Crusaders revived Jericho, building a castle here, but after the Crusader kingdom was dissolved, the city declined.

Near Jericho is the seventh century synagogue floor bearing the inscription "Peace upon Israel" and the ruins of the synagogue at Naaran, at the fertile oasis created by the springs of Ein Duk and Ein Nueima. An aqueduct from Ein Nueima carried water to Hisham's Palace, or Khirbet Mafjar, the eighth century winter palace of Caliph Hisham ibn Abd el-Malik.

The excavated tel ▼

The stone of Temptation, on which Jesus is said to have sat.

The Mount of Temptation

The Mount of Temptation ("Quarantel" from the Latin "Mons Quarantana" - Forty Days) looms behind Old Jericho in the west. A stony path ascends the hill and leads to the Greek monastery carved out of the mountain-side half-way up and built partly in the rock over the chasm. Here Jesus fasted forty days to resist the devil's offer to him of "all the kingdoms in the world" (Luke 4:5).

Interior of the Church

"*And immediately the Spirit driveth him into the wilderness. And He was there in the wilderness forty days, tempted of Satan: and was with the wild beasts: and the angels ministered unto him.*"

Mark 1:12

The Mount of Temptation (Jebel Quarantel)

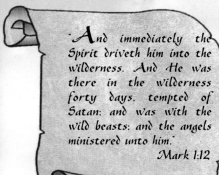

Hisham's Palace

Many rulers spent their winters in Jericho, enjoying its mild climate. The ruins of a magnificent two-storied palace, two miles north of ancient Jericho at Khirbet al-Mafjar, were excavated in 1935-36. An Arab inscription bearing the name "Hisham" identified the ruins as belonging to an elaborate winter resort of the tenth Ummayad Caliph Walid I of Damascus, who ruled from 724 to 743.

It has a pillared courtyard, two mosques and two bath-houses with perfectly preserved mosaic floors. In the guest room is an exquisite mosaic carpet depicting a lion stalking three fawns nibbling at a dark-green tree. The palace was destroyed by an earth-quake four years after it was built.

Part of the mosaic floor of a sixth-seventh century synagogue depicting an anonymous Aramaic inscription reading "Shalom al Yisrael" ("Peace over Israel") with a holy ark, a seven branched menorah and ram's horn (shofar). ▼

▲ *Jericho, as depicted in the Byzantine mosaic Madaba map.*

◀ *Plastered skull from pre-pottery Neolithic Jericho (6000 B.C.), Jordan Archaeological Museum, Amman.*

Bird's eye view of Hisham's Palace ▼

▼ *Complex of palaces from Herodian periods on both banks of Wadi Kelt.*

Greek Orthodox procession near the Monastery of St. John the Baptist on the way to the baptismal site on the Jordan River.

▼ Pilgrims participating in a ceremony at the spot where Jesus was baptized in the River Jordan.

" Jesus was baptized
by John in the Jordan."

Mark 1:9

▲ The baptismal site on the Jordan River

Baptismal Site on the River Jordan.

The traditional site of baptism on the Jordan is miles east of Jericho. The Emperor Constantine's mother, Helena, ordered two churches built near the Jordan, one in honor of John the Baptist and the other dedicated to the prophet Elijah. Both these churches were destroyed after the Muslim invasion, but the site was again used during the Crusader period. Nearby is the oldest surviving monastery, of St. John the Baptist, which also marks the spot where the Israelites crossed the River Jordan on their way to conquer Jericho. A small octagonal chapel run by the Franciscans lies south of the baptismal site. Many pilgrims come to the site to be baptized during Easter.

A painting of the baptism of Jesus is to be found in the St. John the Baptist Church in Ein Karem. ▼

Monasteries in the Judean Desert

Since time immemorial, the Judean desert has been the main pilgrim route between the biblical towns of Jerusalem and Jericho. Scattered through the gaunt, rocky hillocks are numerous monasteries and churches, usually on Byzantine foundations. One of them is Mar Saba, a Greek Orthodox monastery which no woman is permitted to enter and where St. Saba's mummified body is preserved. Another is the Monastery of St. Theodosius where the Three Wise Men - the Magi - rested after paying homage to the infant Jesus. A third is the Monastery of St. George in Wadi Kelt, a gorge which some believe to be the valley of the shadow of death referred to in the 23rd Psalm. The Greek Orthodox monastery of St. George is built on three levels on the slope. The Chapel of the Virgin Mary in the monastery has valuable icons and paintings while the skull of St. George is preserved in the Church of St. John and St. George. Nearby is Elijah's Grotto, where the prophet is said to have lived and been fed by ravens.

Center:
Birds eye view of Nebi Mussa (the prophet Moses), the desert mosque, which, according to Muslim tradition, contains the tomb of Moses.

The Greek Orthodox Monastery of Saint Gerrasimos at Dir Hajlah. ▶

Inn of the Good Samaritan

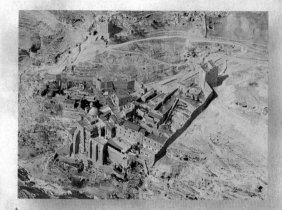

▲ Monastery of Mar Saba in the Judean desert.

Midway between Jerusalem and Jericho in Second Temple times there was a caravanserai, the Inn of the Good Samaritan, scene of the story in Luke 10:30, of how a "certain man went down from Jerusalem to Jericho and fell among thieves". Robbed and injured, he was rescued by a Samaritan who dressed his wounds and carried him to the inn. Ruins of a Turkish khan on the foundations of the Byzantine Monastery of St. Joachim mark the spot.

▼ Mosaic floor in the Martyrius Monastery, Ma'aleh Adoumim

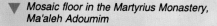

▼ The Inn of the Good Samaritain

"**A**nd he [the devil] brought him to Jerusalem and set him on a pinnacle of the temple, and said unto him. If thou be the Son of God, cast thyself down from hence"

Luke 4:9

▲ The Hulda Steps in the southern wall of the Temple Mount. These led into the courtyard at the time when the Second Temple was standing and were in fact the very steps used by Jesus.

▼The Pinnacle of the Temple in Jerusalem to which Satan brought Jesus in order to tempt him for the third time.

The Dead Sea

Floating on the southern part of the Dead Sea.

Salt "pillars" and accumulation of minerals.

The Dead Sea, the name by which this large salt lake is commonly known, is the lowest spot on earth, 1290 feet below sea-level. Measuring 48 miles in length and 11 miles across, the curious oily feel of the lake water is due to its high solids contents (30%). These are in the form of salts, the most important being magnesium, sodium, calcium, potassium chlorides and magnesium bromide. These are refined and processed and then utilized

"And from the plain to the Sea of Chinneroth on the east, and unto the sea of the plain, even the Salt Sea on the east."
Joshua 12:3

"And their south border was from the shore of the Salt Sea, from the bay that looketh southward."
Joshua 15:2

for industrial and agricultural purposes. The percentage of salts in the Dead Sea is over ten times that in ocean water.

Already in biblical times the Sea was called by several names - the Salt Sea (Gen14:3), the Sea of the Aravah or Plain (Joshua 3:16), the East Sea (Ezechiel 4:16) and the Former Sea (Zech. 14:8). Josephus called it the Sea of Asphalt and in the Talmud it is mentioned as the Sea of Salt and the Sea of Sodom.

The Sea has no outlet yet such is the heat of the valley that, due to evaporation, even at the time of the greatest floods the lake does not rise more than a few feet. Modern research has proved that the Dead Sea exists in almost the same form and area as in the time of Abraham. However, in recent decades the water-line has retreated due to drought and over-exploitation by both Israel and Jordan. Bathing in the waters is a

"*But his wife looked back from behind him. and she became a pillar of salt.*"

Genesis 19:26

The rock-pillar known as "Lot's Wife".

Sunrise over the Dead Sea

Mount Sodom ▶

curious experience. Everyone floats and a non-swimmer cannot drown so long as he keeps his head up.

The appearance of the lake does not fulfil the impression conveyed by its popular name. "The Dead Sea", said an ancient traveler, "did not strike me with that sense of desolation and dreariness which I suppose it ought. I thought it a pretty, smiling lake, a nice ripple on the surface". At sunrise and sunset it is astonishingly beautiful but the occasional smell of sulphur, the dreary salt marsh at the southern end, the dead driftwood and the absence of fish and almost all organic life do indeed explain the name.

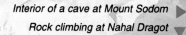

Interior of a cave at Mount Sodom ▶
Rock climbing at Nahal Dragot ▼

Qumran

The heaped-up ruins of Qumran at the foot of bleak, cavern-pitted cliffs aroused no particular attention until 1947, when two Bedouin shepherd boys found seven earthenware jars containing price-less biblical manuscripts. Sensing that they might have monetary value, the Bedouins took some of the linen-wrapped rolls to Bethlehem. Further searches uncovered a wealth of parchment fragments and scrolls which were hidden two thousand years ago. The ancient community of Qumran was described by Josephus, Pliny and Philo and has been identified with the Essenes, a monastic brotherhood which devoted itself to asceticism. They probably lived in caves and tents and were celibate. Ritual purification

The Caves of Qumran ▲

Birds eye view of Qumran ▼

The Dead Sea

Reservoir

The watch-tower

Pantry

One of the great cisterns

The caves

was an essential part of their lives and a system of water cisterns and dams was able to hold vast amounts of water. The hierarchical community was led by the Teacher of Righteousness and its members believed they were the Chosen. Some of their teachings were similar to those of the early Christians. However whereas their main doctrine was their exclusivity and the focus on the end of days, Jesus was concerned with ordinary man and a new age.

Among the treasures found was the unique Copper Scroll, describing the Temple treasures and listing the places of their

The entrance to one of the caves, discovered ▲
in the summer of 1952

The caves of Qumran ▼

▲ Two fragments
from the Dead Sea
Scrolls found at Qumran
with an inkpot
of the Roman period.

▲ One of the great cisterns.

concealment, and the Temple Scroll about the Temple itself. Some of the scrolls contain the oldest existing Old Testament texts. Apart from the Book of Esther, parts of all books were found as well as some books of the Apocrypha, showing that the texts have not basically changed in two thousand years. Other scrolls are sectarian works describing the sect's code of ethics and beliefs. One of the most fascinating describes the War between the Sons of Darkness and Light before the start of the Messianic Age. Some of the scrolls are housed in the Shrine of the Book in the Israel Museum.

When the ruins were cleared in 1951, a complete Essene monastery of the second and first centuries B.C. were found. This included a large assembly hall and dining room, kitchens, laundry, a potters' kiln, cisterns, ritual baths, a cemetery and a scriptorium with bronze inkwells where the Essenes copied the already ancient manuscripts. It is thought that they hid them and the rest of their library when the Romans were at their gates. These documents remained hidden for 2000 years.

▲ Cracked steps leading to a ritual bath, caused by the earthquake of 31 B.C.

The watch-tower ▼

The excavated ruins of the buildings that stood here before the place was abandoned in the first century A.D.
▼

Ein Gedi

The biblical oasis of Ein Gedi, fed by fresh water springs, is the place to which David withdrew with his men in his flight from Saul. King Saul was told that David and his men were in the wilderness of En-Gedi, and "he took three thousand men and went to seek David upon the rocks of the wild goats" (1 Samuel 24:1-4).

In the days of King Solomon, Ein Gedi was famed for its fragrant "camphire in the vineyards of Engedi" (Song of Solomon 1:14) and archaeological digs have indeed revealed ancient perfume vats.

Falling from a 300 feet high cliff is a waterfall whose waters, cascading through the gorge and creating several other waterfalls, afford a luxuriant growth of semi-tropical vegetation. The deep gorge is called "Nahal David" (David's brook). Here wild goats (ibex) continue to roam freely and undisturbed to this day.

In 1949 a kibbutz was established on this border - it was then on the edge of the Green Line between Israel and Jordan - and today it has a Field School and a popular Guest House. Nearby, the spa of Hamei Ein Gedi is famous for its thermo-mineral waters, which have unique chemical properties. The source of the waters is in ancient lakes whose waters infiltrated the depths, passing through rocks and causing chemical changes. On their way to the surface, the rising waters mix with the waters of the Dead Sea resulting in their special composition. The most important mineral is sulphur, which is found in higher concentration here than anywhere else in the world. At this spa, sufferers of psoriasis, arthritis, rheumatism and other bone and muscle ailments can alleviate their aches and pains. Solomon, Herod and Cleopatra also took cures in the area.

At Nahal David

The ancient ▶ synagogue

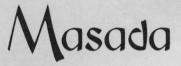

Aerial view
of the northern palace
with its three levels.

Masada

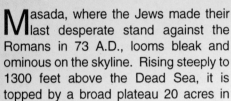

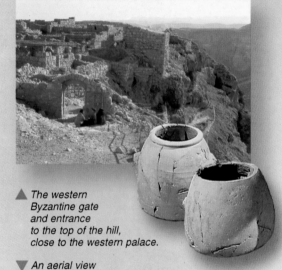

The western
Byzantine gate
and entrance
to the top of the hill,
close to the western palace.

An aerial view
of the fortress-hill of Masada

Masada, where the Jews made their last desperate stand against the Romans in 73 A.D., looms bleak and ominous on the skyline. Rising steeply to 1300 feet above the Dead Sea, it is topped by a broad plateau 20 acres in size which carried Herod's magnificent constructions and where the drama of the final revolt was played out.

First fortified by the Hasmoneans as one of their line of defence bastions, holding back invasion from the east, it was rebuilt by Herod, making it virtually impregnable. Massive fortifications, palaces and storehouses were designed to protect Herod in case of protracted war and he built hanging gardens, a swimming pool, an elaborate bath-house, vast stores, a synagogue and ritual baths, protecting the whole by sentry towers set at intervals along an encircling wall. Approach was difficult. The only way seems to have been by the narrow Snake Path, tortuously winding up the eastern slope of the mountain, from where can be seen the threatening outlines

The excavated and partially-restored store-houses.

A beautiful mosaic from the Byzantine church. ▷

▽ Northwestern corner of apodyterium with basin built by Zealots

▲ The caldarium (hot room) in the bath-house adjoining the northern palace.

The Byzantine church built on Masada in the 6th century A.D.
▽

of the Roman camp at the base of the hill. After the fall of Jerusalem in 70 A.D., a group of 960 Jewish zealots - men, women and children, barricaded themselves on Masada and held it for three years. When conquest seemed imminent and the Romans were ready to burst in, Josephus tells us that the commander, Eleazar ben Yair, spoke to the defenders enjoining each man to kill his family. Then they "chose ten men by lot to slay all the rest... and when these ten had slain them all, they made the same rule for casting lots for themselves" (Wars of the Jews, Book VII:9:1). When the Romans eventually entered the fortress, they found ample stores to show that it was not lack of provisions that caused the surrender; otherwise they found nothing but piles of corpses and a deathly silence.

Masada can be reached by climbing the Snake Path, by taking the easier ascent along the Roman ramp on the west slope, or by taking the cable car. On the site are relics of Herod's luxurious living, contrasting sharply with the simple ovens and earthenware cooking pots of the Zealots. The magnificent three-tiered norther palace, the Roman bath-house with its heating system, the storehouses and the magnificent mosaics of the western palace, the columbarium - possibly for the nesting of carrier pigeons for communication, and the Byzantine chapel can all be visited.

On summer evenings, the tragedy is enacted in a sound-and-light program telling the epic of Masada and its heroic defenders, of their last days and the final consuming fires.

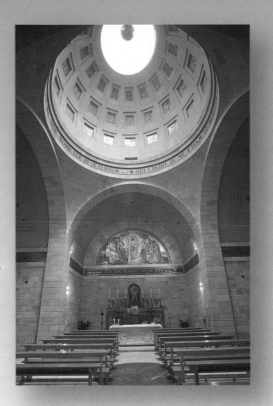

Jesus eating in Bethany at the house of Simon the Leper.

Bethany

Known in Arabic as el-Azariye, Bethany was the home of Lazarus and his sisters Martha and Mary. Here Mary "sat at Jesus' feet, but Martha was cumbered about much serving". Complaining to Jesus that Mary did not help her, Martha was told "that Mary hath chosen that good part, which shall not be taken away from her" (Luke 10:39-40).

Lazarus became ill and died and when he had been dead for four days, Jesus came from the River Jordan on his way to Jerusalem and restored him to life. Lazarus' grave is behind the Franciscan Sanctuary of St. Lazarus, a masterpiece built in 1954 by the Italian architect Barluzzi, which incorporates fourth, sixth and twelfth century remains. In the church are many mosaics, copies of frescoes

▲ *The interior of the Church of Lazarus*
▼ *The Church of Lazarus*

painted by G. Vagarini. Above the church is a ruined tower said to be on the site of Simon the Leper's house, where Jesus sat when a woman anointed him with precious spikenard, and his fellow guests complained of the waste: "Why trouble ye the woman?". And Jesus said, "For she hath wrought good work upon me" (Mat. 26:10).

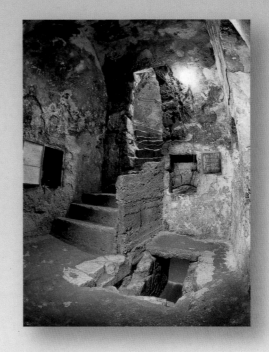

▲ The tomb of Lazarus ▼

" ...A certain man was sick, named Lazarus, of Bethany, the town of Mary and her sister Martha... when Jesus came, he found that he had lain in the grave four days already.... he cried with a loud voice, Lazarus, come forth. And he that was dead came forth, bound hand and foot with grave-clothes."

John 11:1-43

▼ A mill-stone in the Church of St. Lazarus

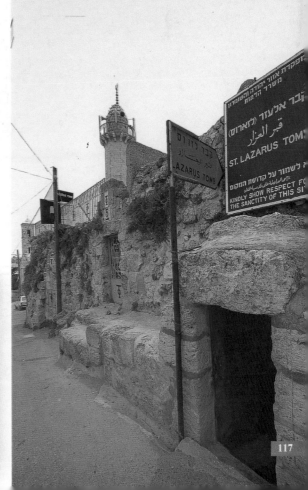

▲ The Palm Sunday procession starting from Bethphage on its way to Jerusalem

"*And when they drew nigh unto Jerusalem, and were come to Bethphage, unto the mount of Olives*"

Matthew 21:1

▼ The Church of Bethphage

▲ A fresco showing a Palm Sunday Procession in the Crusader Chapel at Bethphage, the Mount of Olives (XII Cent.)

Bethphage

Bethphage, "house of figs", on the slopes of the Mount of Olives, is closely associated with the last days of Jesus. Here Jesus sent two of his disciples to fetch a young ass for him to ride to make his entrance into Jerusalem amid waving palm branches (Mark 11). It is from here that the Palm Sunday procession begins, ending at the Church of St. Anne in the Old City. In the Church at Bethphage is a stone said to bear the imprint of Jesus' foot as he mounted the ass.

▼ A fresco above the main altar of the church at Bethphage which shows the entry of Jesus into Jerusalem riding on a young ass.

"The Lord shall bless thee out of Zion: and thou shalt see the good of Jerusalem."

Psalm 128:5

Jerusalem

Five thousand years of constant habitation, together with its biblical associations, have made Jerusalem unique.

There is not another city that has been the cause of so many armed conflicts as Jerusalem. Situated on the watershed between the Mediterranean and the Dead Sea, and on the ancient Way of the Patriarchs linking the northern empires to Egypt in the south, it has, from time immemorial, been an important junction - a meeting-place not only of roads but of cultures from the north, south, east and west. Jerusalem itself lies on a triangular plateau about 2500 feet above sea level, creating a pass through the 3000 feet high Hebron-Bethel range. The Temple Mount, or Mount Moriah, constitutes its northern edge, and two smaller hills - Mount Zion on the west and Mount Ophel

on the east - separated by the Tyropoeon Valley, form the south-pointing apex. Because of its proximity to the Gihon Spring, the only fresh-water source in the vicinity, the Canaanites established one of their city-states on narrow Mount Ophel nearly 5000 years ago. Here Abraham met King Melchizedek, "priest of the most high God" (Gen. 14:18). Here was the stronghold of Zion, which in 1000 B.C. was captured by David and transformed into the political and religious capital of the Jews. For fifty shekels of silver, David bought the threshing floor of Araunah the Jebusite just north of Mount Ophel "to build an altar unto the Lord" (II Sam. 24:21). Above this altar Solomon erected the First Temple, thereby turning Jerusalem into a center of pilgrimage. In 586 B.C. the Babylonians burnt down the city and

Temple taking the people into exile; however, fifty years later under Ezra and Nehemiah, Jews were allowed to return and rebuild the Temple. In the first century B.C., Herod the Great made the city into an important capital, building palaces and fortresses and rebuilding the Temple as a magnificent structure. It was this Jerusalem that Jesus knew and here his trial and crucifixion by the Roman rulers took place. The Jewish revolt against the Romans from 66 to 70 A.D. culminated in the destruction of Jerusalem and the Temple by Titus, as foreseen by Jesus, that "there shall not be left here one stone upon another" (Mat. 24:2). Emperor Hadrian rebuilt Jerusalem as a pagan city, Aelia Capitolina. Three centuries of Byzantine rule gave the city a new character and the sixth century Madaba map, discovered in Jordan in 1896, shows its colonnaded streets and fine churches. In 638 the Moslems invaded the city and it became a provincial backwater. Godfrey de Bouillon led the Crusaders into Jerusalem in 1097, massacring all the Jewish and Moslem inhabitants. The Crusaders made it capital of their Latin Kingdom in the twelfth century but were ousted by Saladin in 1187. In 1516 the Mamelukes gained control and were succeeded by the Turks. In 1917, Jerusalem was conquered by General Allenby, and remained under British Mandate rule until 1948. Between 1948-1967, the Old City was under Jordanian rule. Since then, it has been under the sovereignity of the State of Israel and the city has developed into a modern metropolis, preserving its unique character as a holy city.

In today's Jerusalem, multi-storied buildings jostle ancient monumental tombs; modern electric cables and water carriers lie alongside First and Second Temple aqueducts; six-lane highways cross the footpaths trodden by biblical prophets, while Jerusalem's ramparts rise majestically above the bustle of everyday life.

"If I forget thee, O Jerusalem, let my right hand forget her cunning."

Psalm 137:5

"Thus saith the Lord God: This is Jerusalem: I have set it in the midst of the nations and countries that are round about her"

Ezekiel 5:5

St Stephen's Church

Church and Garden of Gethsemane

The Chapel of the Ascension

The Tomb of Mary

Benedictine Sisters

The Church of the Pater Noster

The Russian Compound

Mount of Olives

For Christianity, no mountain holds more far-reaching importance and sentiment than Olivet, or the mount of Olives; nowhere did Jesus spend more time during his mission in Jerusalem. When Jesus was in the area, he would stay with his friends at Bethany and on his way to and from the city he would pass through the Mount of Olives. Here, overlooking the Temple, he taught his disciples, prophesied the destruction of Jerusalem and wept over its fate (Luke 19:37-41). On its slopes, in the Garden of Gethsemane, he was taken captive, and from its summit he ascended. In antiquity, the Mount was indeed covered with olive trees but the Romans cut most of them down to build the rampart for the siege of Jerusalem during the Great Revolt of the Jews in 70 A.D.

The mountain is first mentioned in the Bible when King David, fleeing from Absalom, "went up by the ascent of Mount Olivet "(II Sam. 15:30). During Second Temple times, Jewish pilgrims would bring their red heifers here to be burnt for the ashes of purification (Lev. 16; Heb. 9:13) and signal fires were lit at the new moon to inform Jews of the new month's coming. Here Ezechiel viewed the heavenly chariots and Zechariah prophecied the End of Days: "And his feet shall stand in that day upon the mount of Olives"(Zec. 14:4) ushering in ever lasting peace. Legend tells that the Messiah will enter the Temple Courts through the now-blocked Golden Gate opposite the mountain. For this reason, pious Jews have throughout the ages chosen to be buried here so as to be among the first to follow the Messiah on the Day of Redemption.

From the top of the Mount of Olives there is the most magnificent view of the Old City of Jerusalem, especially at dawn and dusk.

"And David went up by the ascent of mount Olivet, and wept as he went up."
II Samuel 15:30

"Then returned they unto Jerusalem from the mount called Olivet which is from Jerusalem a sabbath day's journey."
Acts 1:12

View of the Mount of Olives in the snow ▶

The Palm Sunday procession starting from Bethphage on its way to Jerusalem.

The Chapel of the Ascension

The Chapel of the Ascension is a small domed octagonal building on the top of the Mount of Olives, marking the traditional spot where Jesus ascended to heaven. A round shrine built over the spot in 380 was partially destroyed by the Persians in 614. It was later reconstructed by the Crusaders, who built a polygonal chapel open to the sky and enclosed by an octagonal wall. The present building, with its finely carved Crusader capitals, is the remains of this church, which was converted to a mosque after Saladin's conquest of Jerusalem in 1187, and its central chapel covered by a cupola. This Chapel was the main architectural inspiration for the Dome of the Rock.

It was here, a Sabbath's day journey away from Jerusalem, that the risen Jesus departed from his disciples, having encountered them forty days after the crucifixion.

Inside is a stone with the impression of a footstep said to have been made by Jesus ascending to heaven. On the Feast of Ascension, forty days after Easter, the different Christian sects hold their ceremonies here.

▲ Inside the Chapel of the Ascension

The Chapel of the Ascension with the white Ascension Tower of the Russian nuns in the background. ▶

▼ *Once a year, on the anniversary of the Ascension, pilgrim ceremonies of various Christians are held in the Chapel.*

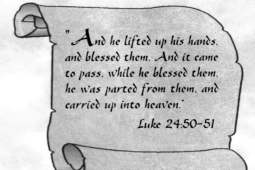

"And he lifted up his hands, and blessed them. And it came to pass, while he blessed them, he was parted from them, and carried up into heaven."

Luke 24:50-51

The Lord's Prayer in Aramaïc

The Church of the Pater Noster

The Eleona, or the Pater Noster Church, was originally erected in the fourth century by Empress Helena, mother of Constantine. A cavern where Jesus taught his disciples the Lord's Prayer is now a chapel and the Carmelite cloister here is lined with glazed tiles bearing the text of the prayer translated into more than sixty languages, including braille.

▲ The Carmelite Chapel, built in 1874, has the Lord's Prayer in 60 languages, the Latin being in bas-relief on the front of the old altar.

▼ The Grotto of the Eschatological Teachings where, according to tradition, Jesus taught the disciples the Lord's Prayer. Here, during the first six centuries, the Patriarchs of Jerusalem were buried.

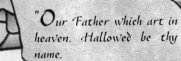

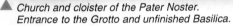

▲ Church and cloister of the Pater Noster.
Entrance to the Grotto and unfinished Basilica.

▼ Cloister of the Pater Noster; the prayer is portrayed on ceramic plaques in more than 60 languages.

"*And when he was come near, he beheld the city and wept over it... For the days shall come upon thee, that thine enemies shall cast a trench about thee...and they shall not leave in thee one stone upon another."*

Luke 19:41-44

Dominus Flevit

One of the Italian architect Antonio Barluzzi's last assignments before his death was the Franciscan chapel of Dominus Flevit, built in 1956 on the ruins of a Byzantine church. Left of the entrance, parts of a fifth century mosaic can still be seen. Here Jesus is said to have wept as he foresaw the doom of Jerusalem and accordingly, the Church is in the shape of a tear. From the chapel, there is a stunning view of the Old City of Jerusalem.

The window above the altar through which the Temple Mount and Jerusalem can be seen.

The Church of Dominus Flevit on the slopes of the Mount of Olives, facing the Temple Mount.

Ossuary in Dominus Flevit

▲ *Interior of the Church*

The Russian Church of Mary Magdalene

The White Russian onion-turreted Church of Mary Magdalene was built in 1888 by Czar Alexander III in memory of his mother. The gold domes are typical of the Muscovite church style.

Gethsemane and the Basilica of the Agony

The Basilica of the Agony and the Russian Orthodox Church on the slopes of the Mount of Olives.

On the lower slopes of the Mount of Olives there stands to this day a stately grove of eight ancient olive trees. These trees and their fruit have given this site its name, Gethsemane: gat-shamna is olive-press in Aramaic. The garden is well-kept by the Franciscan brothers. It was here at Gethsemane that Jesus came with his disciples to pray. Here he grew despondent and was tempted to find a way out, only

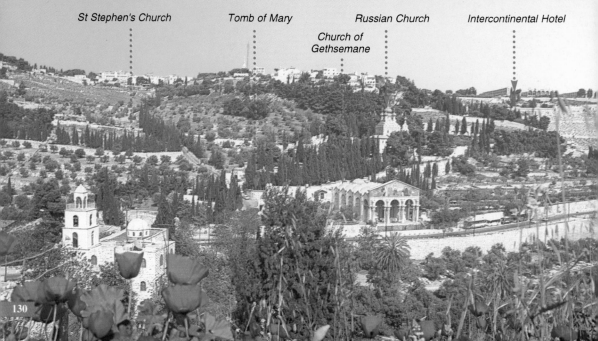

St Stephen's Church　　　Tomb of Mary　　　Russian Church　　　Intercontinental Hotel

Church of Gethsemane

Angel from Gethsemane

finally to overcome the weakness of the flesh and accept the Divine Will. Betrayed by Judas, Jesus was arrested here by the soldiers of the High Priest and taken away for indictment.

The focal point of the garden is the Basilica of the Agony, its blue and gold mosaic pediment visible from afar. Also known as the Church of All Nations, for it was sponsored jointly by several countries, it was erected by Barluzzi in 1924 over the remains of two earlier churches, one from Byzantine and one from Crusader times. The mosaic on the front facade by Bargelli depicts Christ offering up both his and the world's

The Rock of Agony

The cupola of the Church of All Nations. ▼

The Golden Gate

sufferings: "...with a strong cry and tears, offering up prayers and supplications was heard for his reverence" (Heb. 5:7). Beneath the mosaic, and standing upon the columns, are the four evangelists, Matthew, Mark, Luke and John.

Within the church, in front of the main altar, is the traditional Rock of the Agony upon which Jesus prayed and sweated blood the night before his arrest. The rock is surrounded by a crown of thorns of wrought iron. Above the altar is a painting depicting an angel comforting Jesus.

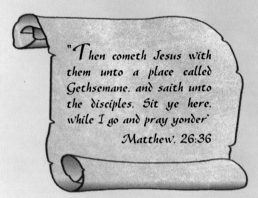

"Then cometh Jesus with them unto a place called Gethsemane. and saith unto the disciples. Sit ye here. while I go and pray yonder"

Matthew. 26:36

Ancient olive trees in the
Garden of Gethsamene

▲ The Church of the Tomb of the Virgin Mary ▼

The Church of the Tomb of the Virgin Mary

A majestic staircase descends to the crypt where Mary was buried and then taken up to heaven. This candle-lit cave, which was built by the Crusaders, is today in the hands of the Armenian and Greek Orthodox churches. In the church are altars dedicated to Joachim and Anne, the Virgin Mary's parents. Queen Melisanda, who reigned here during the Crusader period, is also buried here.

The Kidron Valley
Valley of Jehoshaphat

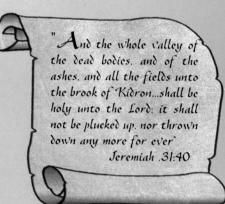

"*And the whole valley of the dead bodies, and of the ashes, and all the fields unto the brook of Kidron...shall be holy unto the Lord: it shall not be plucked up, nor thrown down any more for ever*"
Jeremiah 31:40

Between the Mount of Olives and the Temple Mount lies the Kidron Valley, sometimes called the Valley of Jehoshaphat for the fourth king of Judah. Here is a row of Second Temple monumental sepulchers, including the so-called Absalom's tomb, named after David's son who erected a pillar in his honor since he had no children to remember him (II Sam. 18:18). In the mausoleum of Bnei Hezir are the remains of the priestly family mentioned in I Chronicles 24:15. It is also known as the Tomb of St. James for Jesus' brother who, according to tradition, was killed by the high priest and buried here.

The Tomb of Absalom

The Tomb of Bnei Hezir

The Tomb of Zacharias

The Rockefeller Museum was founded in 1927 thanks to a generous donation by the American millionaire John D. Rockefeller. It houses an excellent collection of archaeological finds and has fascinating reconstructions of a seventh-century Ommayad palace and baths.

Mt. Scopus

Mount Scopus, the northern extension of the Mt. of Olives, is one of the most strategic heights around Jerusalem. Josephus Flavius writes how Roman general Cestius Gallus "pitched his camp on Scopus" (Wars 2:19:4), then Titus and later the Crusaders also stationed their troops there. More recently, after the War of Independence, the Israelis remained in possession of the Hebrew University and Hadassah hospital on Mt. Scopus but the road link with the rest of Jerusalem was cut. Only during the 1967 Six-Day War was it re-taken.   Since then, both institutions have been rebuilt and are among the finest and most modern the world over. On the outskirts of the University is the Augusta Victoria Hospital. Built in 1910, it was the residence of the British Governor-General from the end of World War I until 1927. Its square pointed tower is a Jerusalem landmark.

▲ *The Rockefeller Museum*

▼ *The Hebrew University's amphitheater with the Judean desert in the background.*

▲ *View of the Hebrew University, founded in 1925 on Mount Scopus.* ▼

Mount Zion - David's Tomb

"For out of Zion shall go forth the law and the word of the Lord from Jerusalem"

Isaiah. 2:3

"For the Lord hath chosen Zion: he hath desired it for his habitation."

Psalm 132:13

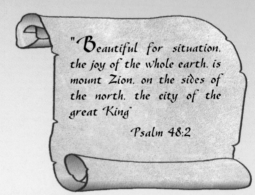

The traditional Tomb of King David

Due to a fourth century mistaken geographical identification, Mt. Zion was attributed to its present site on the western hill, though in fact the Zion of the Old Testament is identical with the city of David on the eastern hill: "David took the strong hold of Zion: the same is the city of David" (II Sam.5:7). By Jesus' time, nearly one thousand years later, a monument to David's tomb had migrated to the present Mt. Zion. The tomb fell into ruin in 133 A.D, but was accidentally rediscovered in 1158 and is venerated to this day by Jews, Christians and Moslems.

"Beautiful for situation, the joy of the whole earth, is mount Zion, on the sides of the north, the city of the great King"

Psalm 48:2

Zion Gate

Mount Zion and the Old City Wall

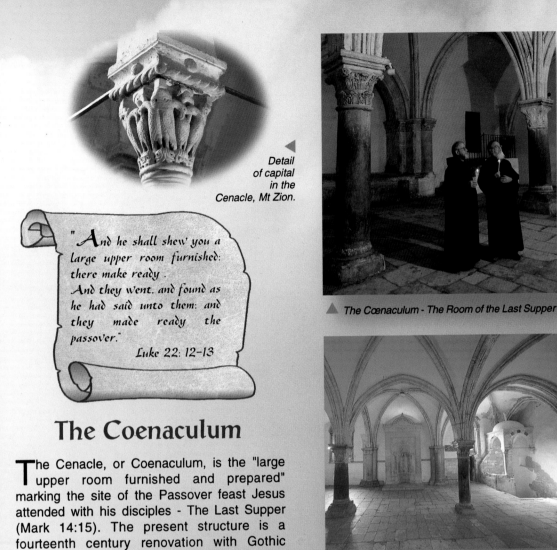

Detail
of capital
in the
Cenacle, Mt Zion.

▲ The Cœnaculum - The Room of the Last Supper

" *And* he shall shew you a
large upper room furnished:
there make ready .
And they went. and found as
he had said unto them: and
they made ready the
passover."
Luke 22: 12-13

The Coenaculum

The Cenacle, or Coenaculum, is the "large upper room furnished and prepared" marking the site of the Passover feast Jesus attended with his disciples - The Last Supper (Mark 14:15). The present structure is a fourteenth century renovation with Gothic windows and Crusader arches. Below the Cenacle is the "Hall of the Washing of the Feet", where Jesus poured "water into a basin, and began to wash the disciples' feet" (John 13:5). Every year before Easter, the ceremony of foot-washing is re-enacted by the various Christian sects and the highest prelate of each church washes the feet of some of his clergy.

▼ The Church of the Hagia Maria Zion

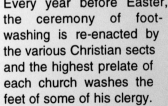

The Church of Hagia Maria Zion
The Dormition

The octagonal Church of Hagia Maria Zion, also know as the Church of the Dormition, towers above Mount Zion and commemorates the tradition that here Mary, mother of Jesus, fell into eternal sleep. In 383, the Byzantines built the Church of the Column here, placing the flagellation post within it. In 415, John II, Bishop of Jerusalem, enlarged this church, calling it Hagia Sion - Holy Zion. It is this church, also called the mother of all churches, that is shown on the sixth century Madaba map found in Jordan. The Hagia Zion Church was destroyed in 614 by the Persians and rebuilt by the Crusaders who named it Our Lady of Mt. Zion, incorporating in it the Room of the Last Supper. This church was also destroyed in 1219. In 1517 the Turks turned it into a

▼ *The crypt*

mosque. The present church was built at the beginning of the twentieth century by German Benedictines on land given to Kaiser Wilhelm II during his visit to the Holy Land, and the church and abbey are still run by Benedictine monks. The beautiful mosaic floor in the church depicts the Holy Trinity, the apostles and the zodiac. A staircase leads from the upper church to the crypt venerated as Mary's home after the Resurrection of Jesus and as the place of her death. In the center of the crypt is a life-size statue of the sleeping Mary made of cherry wood and ivory and in the dome above, a mosaic depicting the figure of Christ welcoming his mother, surrounded by six famous women of the Old Testament.

Aerial view of Mount Zion with the Hagia Maria Zion Church and King David's Tomb. At the center left, the ancient reservoir now called the Sultan's Pool. Above it, the red-roofed houses of the nineteenth century neighborhood of Yemin Moshe and modern west Jerusalem.

▼

The Dormition Sanctuary

The Hagia Maria Zion Sanctuary

The Church of St. Peter in Gallicantu

The Church of St. Peter in Gallicantu stands on the generally accepted site of the House of Caiaphas, High Priest at the time of Jesus' execution. Here Peter is said to have denied his master, according to Jesus' prophecy that, "Before the cock crow, thou shalt deny me thrice" (Luke 22:61). A Maccabean stairway connecting Mount Zion to the Gihon Spring can still be seen, and excavations have revealed inscriptions and weights and measures of Second Temple times, as well as a rock-cut flagellation post.

▲ The Church of St. Peter in Gallicantu

"And Peter said. Man. I know not what thou sayest. And immediately while he yet spake. the cock crew. And the Lord turned. and looked upon Peter. And Peter remembered the word of the Lord. how he had said unto him. 'Before the cock crow.' thou shalt deny me thrice. And Peter went out. and wept bitterly".

Luke 22:60–62

The mosaic-adorned interior of the Church of St. Peter ▼ in Gallicantu

The City of David

Excavations on the site of David's city have brought to light part of the Jebusite ramparts of 4000 years ago, Israelite houses and fortifications from the time of King David, as well as later walls and towers.

An ancient flight of steps leads up to the church and is believed to be those trodden by Jesus on his way to be tried at the House of Caiphas. The site is commemorated by the church.

An artist's impression of the southern spur or ridge on which David built his city, looking to the northeast. The city walls shown are those built by Hezekiah in the eighth century B.C. for defence against the Assyrians. These walls were rebuilt under the Hasmoneans in the 2nd and 1st centuries B.C. From the time of Solomon, Jerusalem grew gradually to the north and west.

A Hebrew inscription, on display at the Istanbul Archaeological Museum, describes the construction of Hezekiah's Tunnel.

The Siloam Tunnel

"And said unto him, Go, wash in the Pool of Siloam. He went his way therefore, and washed, and came seeing.

John 9:7

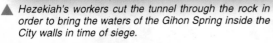

▲ Hezekiah's workers cut the tunnel through the rock in order to bring the waters of the Gihon Spring inside the City walls in time of siege.

▼ The Pool of Siloam.

In biblical times, the Gihon Spring was Jerusalem's only water supply and when enemies were at the gate, the first priority was the safety of the spring. II Chronicles 32:30 tells how King "Hezekiah stopped the upper watercourse of Gihon and brought it straight down to the west side of the city of David". This extraordinary conduit, now known as the Siloam Tunnel or Hezekiah's Tunnel, was dug around 700 B.C. to bring water directly into the town and is still in use. An inscription in ancient Hebrew script found chiselled into the conduit wall, commemorates the meeting of Hezekiah's two work gangs who began at each end of the tunnel and met midway.

At the Pool of Siloam, Jesus healed a man who had been blind from birth and gave him sight (John 9). Empress Eudocia commemorated this miracle with a church built on the spot. It was destroyed in the Persian invasion and to prevent its being rebuilt, the Moslems erected a mosque on the site.

A Hebrew inscription indicating the burial place of Uzziah, King of Judah. The provenance of the inscription on what may have been Uzziah's tombstone is unknown. It is tempting to imagine that it was removed from the royal burial crypt where King David was also buried.

Warren's Shaft

Remains of channels in the City of David, quarried to deliver water to fields in the Kidron Valley

"*David took the castle of Zion, which is the city of David... And he built the city round about*"

I Chronicles 11:5,8

The stepped stone structure that supported a large building in the City of David, perhaps David's palace.

Tower from Second Temple

Achiel House

First wall (Second Temple)

Zion Citadel

Model of the City of David from the Tower of David Museum
Photography: Eli Ne'eman.

Silwan - The City of David, bird's eye view.

The Temple Mount

> *"Then Solomon began to build the house of the Lord at Jerusalem in mount Moriah, where the Lord appeared unto David his father, in the place that David had prepared in the threshing floor of Ornan the Jebusite".*
>
> II Chronicles 3:1

▼ *The Dome of the Rock on the ancient site of the Temple - David Roberts, 1839*

The Temple Mount is traditionally the place where "the Lord God formed man of the dust of the ground" (Gen. 2:7) and where Abraham bound Isaac for sacrifice. It was this same site that David bought from Araunah (Ornan) the Jebusite for fifty shekels of silver, to build an altar to the Lord. His son Solomon took seven years to build a small but lavishly decorated Temple here. Inside, stood the Ark of the Covenant containing the tablets of stone which Moses had received on Mount Sinai (I Kings 6,7). This Temple was destroyed by the Babylonians in 586 B.C. and rebuilt in the same plan on a modest scale fifty years later by the returning exiles. This Temple was in use until the reign of the Seleucid King Antiochus IV who defiled the Temple, thereby sparking the Maccabean revolt in 167 B.C. The festival of Hanukkah commemorates the victory of the

A coin with the facade of the Temple, from the Bar Kokhba Revolt against Rome (AD 132-135).

Maccabees and the rededication of the Temple.

Herod the Great, with his passion for building, doubled the size of the Temple Mount by constructing encasing walls around the sides of the hill and filling the empty parts with vaults over which the platform was laid. Beneath these empty vaults are the so-called Solomon's Stables and other subterranean halls. On this enlarged site, Herod built his magnificent Temple on the same plan as its predecessors, but far larger and grander. This was the Temple where Jesus worshipped and taught. In 70 A.D., the Romans under Titus laid waste to Jerusalem, burning down the Second Temple, and on the site of the Temple built a shrine to Jupiter. During Byzantine times, the Temple Mount was abandoned and when Caliph Omar entered Jerusalem in 638, he found the hilltop refuse-strewn and desolate. Since the same spot was considered to be the scene of Mohammed's miraculous night journey to heaven, and the holiest site of Islam after Mecca and Medina, he cleansed the place and put up a simple wooden mosque.

The Crusaders preserved the importance of the Temple Mount, establishing their headquarters here. The Dome of the Rock was converted into a church called "Templum Domini" (Temple of the Lord) while the El-Aksa Mosque became the residence of the Crusader kings. However, after the Moslems reconquered Jerusalem, the buildings were restored to their former use.

Today, the Temple Mount, which Moslems call Haram al-Sharif - the Noble Enclosure - is studded with shrines from Moslem rulers throughout the centuries. The Dome of the Rock, traditionally built on the spot where the Temple once stood, is one of Jerusalem's main landmarks. Nearby is the Al-Aksa Mosque, the Dome of the Chain, the Dome of the Ascension and the Islamic Museum.

Bird's eye view of the Temple Mount ▼

The Temple

"And as he went out of the temple, one of his disciples saith unto him, *Master, see what manner of stones and what buildings are here! And Jesus answering said unto him, Seest thou these great buildings? There shall not be left one stone upon another, that shall not be thrown down".*

Mark 13:1-2

▲ *A marble relief depicting the golden Menorah and other cult implements of the Temple being carried by Roman soldiers in a triumphal parade in Rome, commemorating Titus' victory over Jerusalem. The Arch of Titus, Rome.*

It was said of Herod's Temple that "he who has not seen the Temple in Jerusalem has never seen a beautiful building". According to the Gospel of John (2:20), it took forty-six years to build and Josephus Flavius, the contemporary historian, said that everything to delight the eye and heart was presented by the outward appearance of the Temple. Here Jesus was presented to the Lord as a baby and his parents went to worship every year at the feast of Passover. When he was twelve, he remained for three days talking to the doctors (Luke 2). The Jews argued with him in Solomon's Porch (John 10); he taught here during the feast of Tabernacles, and at Passover he overturned the moneychangers' tables. When Jesus died, "the veil of the temple was rent in twain from the top to the bottom" (Matthew 27:51), and, as he had prophesied, when the Temple was destroyed in the year 70, not one stone remained upon another.

The Temple was built in the tenemos style, with a graduated approach to the increasingly sacred areas. Gentiles were not allowed beyond the outermost plaza, whilst the sacred Holy of Holies could be entered only by the High Priest, only on the holiest day of the year, the Day of Atonement. The sacrificial altar stood in front of the Holy of Holies and animals, meal and wine were continuously offered. The Priests and Levites maintained the precinct and thousands of people visited daily.

Model of the Second Temple, ▼

The Dome of the Rock

The Dome of the Rock, traditionally the site of Mohammed's ascent to heaven on his winged steed, is set on the actual bedrock of the highest point of the Temple Mount. The Muslim Caliph Abd-el Malik built this superb structure in 691, partly to rival the Church of the Holy Sepulcher. The harmony of its proportions and its magnificent decorations are remarkable, especially the roof, which was gold-plated in 1994. The octagonal structure is similar in form and artistic origin to St. Peter's house in Capernaum, and its Byzantine-style decorations were executed by the many Byzantine artisans still living in the city at the time of its construction. It has been renovated many times, notably in the reign of Suleiman the Magnificent who replaced the mosaics with tiles. There are four doors leading into the Dome of the Rock. Eight marble pillars and sixteen columns support the wooden ceiling, which is richly decorated with stucco painted in red and gold. The mosaic decorations and arches are all from the original construction, as are the inscriptions from the Koran in the cupola. The stained-glass windows are from the renovations made by Suleiman the Magnificent.

In the center of the building, beneath the dome, is the Rock where, according to Islamic tradition, Ishmael, not Isaac, was to be sacrificed, and from where Mohammed ascended to heaven on his Night Journey, though Jerusalem is not mentioned in the Koran. Next to the rock is a tower-shaped urn said to contain two hairs from the beard of the Prophet Mohammed. A cavity in the Rock opens on to the grotto beneath known as the Well of the Souls, where the souls of the dead gather to pray.

▲ *The interior of the Dome of the Rock*

The Dome of the Rock ▼

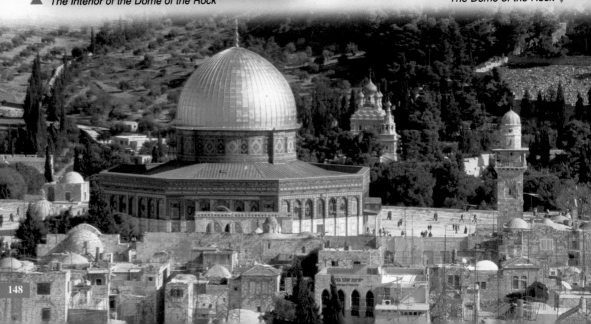

"*Worthy of praise is He who took His servant by night from the Sacred Mosque to the Distant Mosque. the precincts which we have blessed.*"

Koran Soura 17:1

▲ View of the interior of the Dome of the Rock through a fish-eye lens

◄ Detail of the decorations on the outside of the Dome of the Rock

Above right:
One of the five windows
in the Dome of the Rock.

Shrines on the Temple Mount

The Dome of the Chain is so-called because of the chain that hangs from the ceiling. Legend tells that King David sat here to judge the people and if the chain broke in the hands of the accused he was guilty. It may have been the royal treasure houses where funds for building the Dome were kept. The Crusaders used it for prayer and it was known as the Chapel of St. James. The small pillared Dome of the Spirits is on the spot where Mohammed is said to have conversed with Jewish and Christian prophets. Here, it is believed, he will summon the spirits of the faithful on Judgment Day. Another shrine on the Temple Mount is the Dome of Ascension, which is associated with Mohammed's night journey. The Crusaders used it as a baptistry.

There are also many fountains on the Temple Mount - before entering a mosque to pray, Moslems wash their feet. The circular fountain surrounded by trees is called El Kas, The Basin, and is situated over the largest of the underground cisterns on the Temple Mount.

The Islamic Museum

The Islamic Museum is located in a building once known as the Mosque of the Moors and contains a collection of artifacts donated by mosques and other shrines on the Temple Mount. It also has a large collection of illustrated Korans of different periods.

Solomon's Stables

Steps to the east of Al-Aksa lead down to the subterranean vaults called Solomon's Stables. Here the Crusaders kept their horses.

Solomon's stables ▼

The Mosque of El-Aksa

Jerusalem's main mosque is the silver-domed El-Aksa - "the furthest". The original mosque was constructed in the early eighth century by Caliph Walid, son of Ibn el-Malik, who built the Dome of the Rock. Prone to frequent earthquakes, the mosque has often been rebuilt so that there are only a few remains of the original building in the present structure. From 1099-1187, the Crusaders used the Mosque as headquarters of the knights in charge of the Temple area, the Templars, but after the defeat of the Crusaders, Saladdin restored it as a mosque. In the sixteenth century, the inside of the dome was covered with beautiful mosaic and stucco work. Colorful stained glass windows were added , some of which still remain. In 1927 and 1938, after earthquakes, further reconstruction and renovation was carried out.

In 1951, King Abdullah, grandfather of the late King Hussein, was assassinated at the entrance to the mosque and in 1969 an arsonist destroyed a priceless 1,000 year old wood and ivory "minbar" (pulpit) which Saladdin had installed some 800 years before.

The distinctive seven-arched entrance porch dates from the thirteenth century.

Interior of the Mosque of El Aksa ▼

The Church of St Anne & Pools of Bethesda

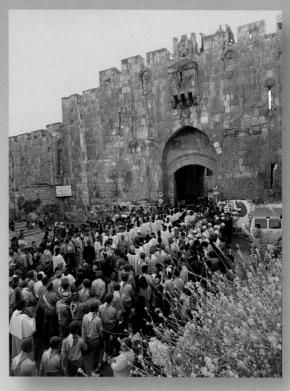

The Crusader Church of St. Anne was built in 1140, on the remains of a Byzantine Church, to commemorate the traditional site of Mary's birthplace at the home of her parents Anne and Joachim. When Saladdin conquered Jerusalem, he turned the building into an Islamic school but after the Ottoman conquest, it was abandoned. Today, the White Fathers use it as a Greek Seminary. In the crypt is a small cave said to the birthplace of Mary, and above the altar is the figurine of a baby.

In the courtyard of the church of St. Anne is the Pool of Bethesda. Uncovered in 1871, the

▲ *St Stephen's Gate during the Palm Sunday procession*

Mosaic floor of the Byzantine Church *Apsis of Crusader Church* *St. Anne's Church* *Byzantine Church*

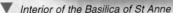
Statue of Anne and Mary ◄

Vessel for Holy Water ►

pool appears as a deep pit broken by a series of stone foundations and archways. Used as a rain catchment pool during Herod's reign, it was part of a grandiose plan to augment Jerusalem's meager water supply. It was here that Jesus miraculously cured the infirm man on the Sabbath.

(John 5:1-13).

▼ Interior of the Basilica of St Anne

Interior of the Basilica of St Anne - The main altar ▼

Via Dolorosa

1 - Church of Gethsemane
    (Church of All Nations).
2 - Tomb of the Virgin.
3 - Church of St. Stephen.
4 - St. Stephen's Gate
    (Lions' Gate).
5 - Birthplace of the
    Virgin Mary,
    Greek Orthodox Convent
    of the Saints Joachim
    and Anna.
6 - Church of Saint Anne,
    Greek Catholic Seminary.
    Birthplace of the Virgin Mary
    and Pool of Bethesda.
7 - Birkat Israel.
8 - Pilgrims' meeting place.
9 - Sanctuaries of the Flagellation
    and Condemnation
    (Second Station).
10 - El Omariye School (First Station).
11 - Notre Dame de Sion Convent
    of Ecce Homo
    Lithostrotos.
12 - Prison of Christ
13 - Armenian Catholic Patriarch
    Church of Our Lady of the Spasm.
14 - Church of the Redeemer
15 - Church of the Holy Sepulcher.

The traditional Friday procession along the Via Dolorosa

The Via Dolorosa, "Way of Sorrow" or "Way of the Cross" is Christendom's most sacred route. It is the path followed by Jesus from the judgment court, the praetorium, to Golgotha, the place of the Crucifixion, bearing the Cross on his back.

Every Friday at 3 p.m., Christian pilgrims from all over the world join the Franciscan procession to retrace these steps and recall Jesus' Agony.

There are fourteen stations on the Way of the Cross, nine along the narrow street and five inside the Church of the Holy Sepulcher. All are marked by chapels or churches for meditation and prayer. Despite the hustle and bustle of the route, it is a moving spiritual experience to wander along the Way where Jesus suffered on his last day on earth 2000 years ago.

The Praetorium in the courtyard of the Al-Omariya school.

"*Then Pilate therefore took Jesus and scourged him.*"
John 19:1

"*Then delivered he him therefore unto them to be crucified. and they took Jesus and led him away.*"
John 19:16

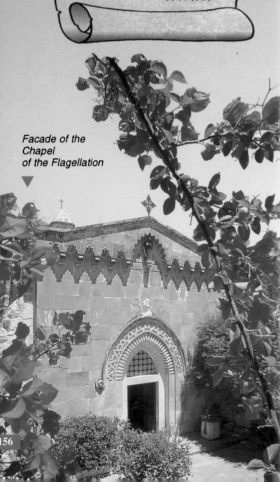

Facade of the Chapel of the Flagellation

The Stations of the Cross

◆ 1st Station ───────────
Jesus is condemned.

It was in the Praetorium, in the Antonia Fortress, the headquarters of the Roman garison stationed in Jerusalem, that Jesus was tried by Pontius Pilate and condemned. The First Station on the Via Dolorosa is today in the courtyard of the The Al Omariya school.

"*And straightaway in the morning the chief priests held a consultation with the elders and scribes and the whole council. and bound Jesus and carried him away. and delivered him to Pilate.*"
Mark 15:1

◆ 2nd Station ───────────
Jesus takes up the Cross

The Franciscan Chapel of the Flagellation and Chapel of Condemnation commemorate the sites where Jesus was scourged and given the Cross to bear.

"*And the soldiers platted a crown of thorns. and put it on his head. and they put on him a purple robe. and said. Hail. king of the Jews! And they smote him with their hands.*"
John 19:2-3

Interior of the Dome of the Convent of the Flagellation.

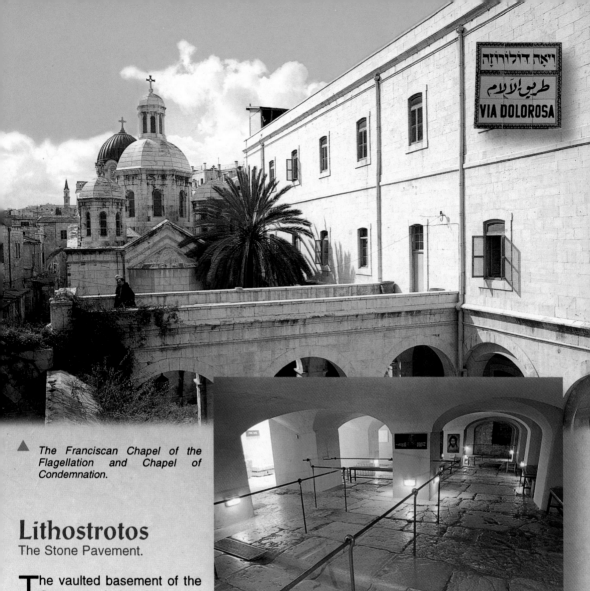

VIA DOLOROSA
דיאה דולורוזה
طريق الآلام

▲ The Franciscan Chapel of the Flagellation and Chapel of Condemnation.

Lithostrotos
The Stone Pavement.

The vaulted basement of the Convent of the Sisters of Zion covers the remains of a Roman pavement, Lithostrotos, made of large flagstones specially etched to prevent horses from slipping. It was once thought that this was part of the Antonia Fortress, however it probably dates back to the time of the Emperor Hadrian and was the forum of the Aelia Capitolina, as Hadrian named Jerusalem in the second century. On the paving stones are signs of the 'Game of the King' played by the Roman soldiers. Beneath the Lithostrotos, a subterranean cistern for collecting water has been discovered. This may have been the Struthion (Ostrich) Pool described by Josephus.

Part of the Pavement in the courtyard of the Antonia Fortress, in the Convent of the "Sisters of Sion". ▲

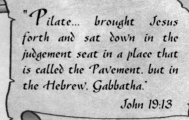

"Pilate... brought Jesus forth and sat down in the judgement seat in a place that is called the Pavement. but in the Hebrew. Gabbatha."
John 19:13

157

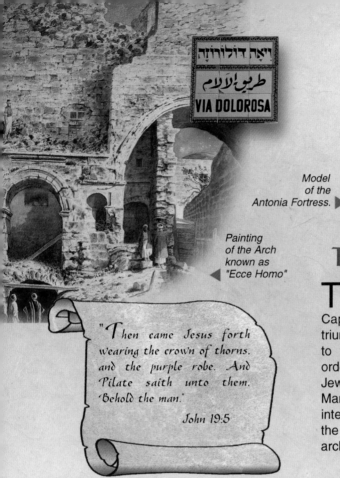

וִיאָה דוֹלוֹרוֹזָה
طريق الآلام
VIA DOLOROSA

Model of the Antonia Fortress. ▶

◀ Painting of the Arch known as "Ecce Homo"

The Ecce Homo Arch

The Ecce Homo arch is part of the eastern entrance to the Roman city Aelia Capitolina, constructed by Hadrian as a triumphal arch with three portals. According to tradition, this is the spot where Pilate ordered Christ to be brought forth to the Jews, proclaiming 'Ecce Homo'- Behold the Man. Today the northern, smaller arch is integrated into the Chapel of Ecce Homo in the Convent of the Sisters of Sion. The large arch spans part of the Via Dolorosa.

"Then came Jesus forth wearing the crown of thorns. and the purple robe. And Pilate saith unto them. 'Behold the man.'

John 19:5

▼ The "Ecce Homo" Chapel

▼ The "Ecce Homo" Arch

◆ 3rd Station
Jesus falls the first time

The sculpture of Thaddeus Zielinsky above the entrance to the Polish chapel on El-Wad Street depicts Jesus falling under the Cross.

"The comforter that should relieve my soul is far from me"

Lamentations 1:16

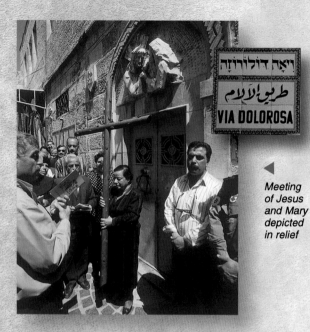

◆ 4th Station

Jesus meets his mother.

The Armenian-Catholic Church of Our Lady of the Spasm marks the spot where the Virgin Mary encountered Jesus. This event is not mentioned in the New Testament.

◄ Meeting of Jesus and Mary depicted in relief

"And Simeon blessed them, and said unto Mary his mother, 'Behold, this child is set for the fall and rising again of many in Israel : and for a sign which shall be spoken against.'

Luke 2:34

◆ 5th Station

The Cyrenian helps Jesus carry the Cross.

The Fifth Station is commemorated by a Franciscan chapel. Here the Way of the Cross begins the ascent to Golgotha.

"And as they led him away, they laid hold upon one Simon, a Cyrenian, coming out of the country, and on him they laid the cross, that he might bear it after Jesus."

Luke 23:26

◄ Entrance to the Fifth Station

◆ 6th Station
The veil of Veronica.

The Church of St. Veronica belonging to the Little Sisters of Jesus probably lies on the site of the house of Veronica, who wiped the blood and dirt from Jesus' face with her veil and the imprint of his face was left on it. The original cloth is kept at St. Peter's Church in Rome. The altar of the church is decorated with a candelabrum of seven branches (Menorah).

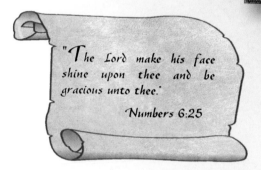

> "*The Lord make his face shine upon thee and be gracious unto thee.*"
>
> *Numbers 6:25*

◆ 7th Station
Jesus falls the second time.

Two chapels connected by a flight of steps mark the site where Jesus fell for the second time under the weight of the Cross. It is believed that on this site was the Gate of Judgment on which the names of the accused and their sentences were posted, and through which Jesus left the city on his way to Golgotha.

> "*And the angel of his presence saved them: In his love and in his pity he redeemed them.*"
>
> *Isaiah 63:9*

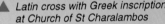
Latin cross with Greek inscription
at Church of St Charalambos

VIA DOLOROSA

◆ 8th Station
Jesus consoles the crying women of Jerusalem.

On the wall of the Greek monastery of St. Charalambos is a stone with a Latin cross and an inscription reading "Jesus Christ is victorious." This station is believed to have been located outside the city walls of Jerusalem in the Second Temple period.

"Jesus turning unto them said. 'Daughters of Jerusalem, weep not for me, but weep for yourselves and for your children."
Luke 23:28

◆ 9th Station
Jesus falls the third time.

A column built into the door of the Coptic church marks the site where Jesus fell for the third time. From this point, he could see the place of crucifixion.

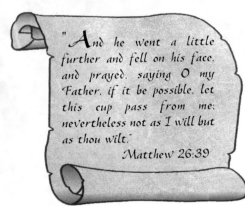
"And he went a little further and fell on his face, and prayed, saying O my Father, if it be possible, let this cup pass from me: nevertheless not as I will but as thou wilt."
Matthew 26:39

The Church
of the
Holy Sepulcher

The Church of the Holy Sepulcher lies in the heart of the Christian Quarter of the Old City. Within the compound is the Hill of Golgotha or Calvary and the Rotunda which contains the Holy Sepulchre. Here Jesus was crucified, buried and resurrected. The Church is maintained by the Roman Catholics, the Greek Orthodox and the Armenians. There are also several chapels including the Chapel of Adam, the Chapel of St. Helena and the Chapel of the Finding of the Cross

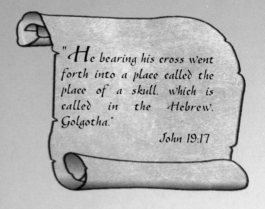

"*He bearing his cross went forth into a place called the place of a skull, which is called in the Hebrew, Golgotha.*"

John 19:17

The Church of the Holy Sepulcher

◆ 10th Station

Jesus is stripped of his garments.

The last five stations of the Way of the Cross are in the Basilica of the Holy Sepulcher. A small stairway of stone leads to the Chapel of the Divestiture.

"*And they gave him to drink wine mingled with myrrh: but he received it not.*"

Mark 15:23

◆ 11th Station

Jesus is nailed to the Cross.

Magnificent mosaics decorate the place where Jesus was crucified before the eyes of his mother. This holy site is guarded by the Roman Catholics.

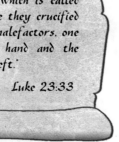

"*And when they were come to the place, which is called Calvary, there they crucified him, and the malefactors, one on the right hand and the other on the left.*"

Luke 23:33

Twelfth Station of the Cross.

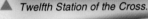

▼ Greek Orthodox altar.

"Jesus when he had cried again with a loud voice, yielded up the ghost."

Matthew 27:50

◆ 12th Station

Jesus dies on the Cross.

A chapel belonging to the Greek Orthodox marks the site of the death of Jesus. The altar is flanked by two supporting pillars and has a silver disk beneath it, marking the exact place where the Cross stood.

Through a cavity in its center can be seen the rock of Golgotha. On each side of the altar are black disks marking the sites of the crosses of the two thieves crucified with Jesus. To the right of the altar is a fissure in the rock believed to have been caused by an earthquake at the time of the death of Jesus: "and the earth did quake and the rocks rent... Now when the centurion, and they that were with him, watching Jesus, saw the earthquake, and those things that were done, they feared greatly, saying, Truly this was the Son of God".

Matthew 27:51,54

This grafiti carved on bedrock beneath the Church of the Holy Sepulcher depicts a ship with a broken mast, and the Latin words "Domine Ivimus", "Lord, we shall go up". It may have been carved in thanksgiving for a safe arrival in Jerusalem by very early Christian pilgrims.

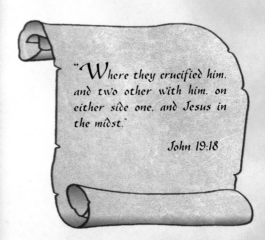

"Where they crucified him, and two other with him, on either side one, and Jesus in the midst."

John 19:18

The Catholic altar dedicated to Our Lady of Dolours stands between the Greek and Latin altars of the Crucifixion on Golgotha. The seventeenth century wooden statue of the Mater Dolorosa was presented by the Queen of Portugal in 1778 and recalls the grief of Mary at the death of Jesus.

◆ 13th Station

Jesus is taken down from the Cross.

An altar marks the spot where Mary received the body of her son after he had been taken down from the Cross. Jesus' body was then laid out on the Stone of Unction (Anointing) and anointed with a mixture of myrrh, aloe and aromatic oils.

▲ *The Stone of Unction*

▼ *Our Lady of Dolours*

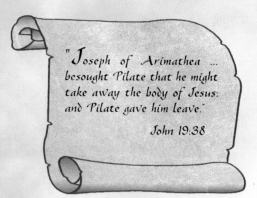

"*Joseph of Arimathea ... besought Pilate that he might take away the body of Jesus; and Pilate gave him leave.*"

John 19:38

The Stone of Unction ▼

The Holy Sepulcher lies in the center of the Rotunda in a richly decorated edicule. The tomb was originally in a cave hewn in the rock, and the Rotunda was built over and around it. The candlesticks and lamps beside the entrance belong to the various denominations and the Greek inscriptions are prayers to the Risen Christ. The first room inside the Sepulcher is the Chapel of the Angel. Here Mary Magdalene, visiting the grave and finding the body gone on the first Sunday after the Crucifixion, saw an angel in white sitting on a stone altar. The pilaster in the center of the room contains a piece of the stone with which the sepulcher of Jesus was closed.

The Chapel of the Angel

"And they saw a young man sitting on the right side, clothed in a long white garment; and they were affrighted"

Mark 16:5

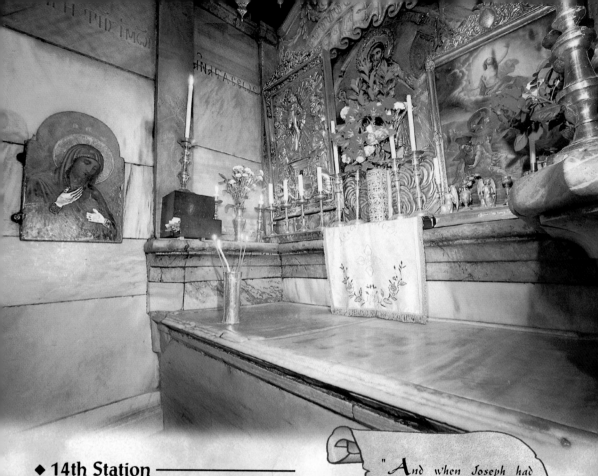

◆ 14th Station

Jesus is placed in the tomb.

The tomb of Jesus, the holiest place in Christendom, lies in the centre of the Church of the Holy Sepulcher beneath the main rotunda, in a beautiful decorative chapel. The sacred rock is covered with marble and above it are paintings depicting the Resurrection.

The Holy Sepulcher itself is covered by a smooth marble slab which has been in place since 1555. Over the Tomb are three reliefs symbolizing the Resurrection, each belonging to one of the principal communities, and 42 lamps burning day and night - thirteen each for the Latins, Greek Orthodox and Armenians and four for the Copts.

> "And when Joseph had taken the body, he wrapped it in a clean linen cloth, and laid it in his own new tomb which he had hewn out in the rock."
>
> Matthew 27:59-60

The Armenian Quarter

The Armenian Quarter is home to a few thousand Armenians, a closely-knit people. Their national home is Armenia - which they believe to be the biblical Ararat - while their spiritual home is the Holy Land. Attached to Jerusalem since 300, when they adopted Christianity a generation before it was accepted by Constantine, the Armenian Compound contains the historic Cathedral and Monastery of St. James, the Armenian Patriarchate and Theological Seminary and a Museum housed in the former Seminary. The Armenians are particularly famous for their colorful ceramic work.

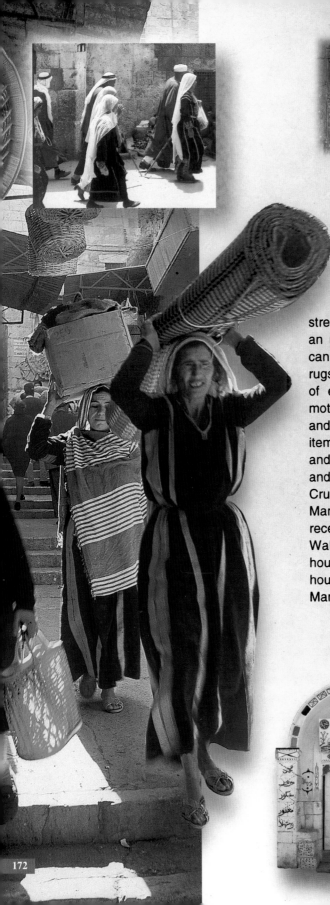

The Moslem Quarter

The Moslem Quarter, by far the largest of the Old City quarters, lies to the north and center of the Old City. The upper stories of its residential sections are densely populated while at street level, its oriental vaulted markets display an unusually broad range of products. Here can be seen colored Hebron glass, handwoven rugs and embroidered dresses, straw baskets of every shape and size, ebony inlaid with mother-of-pearl, leather goods, both folkloric and expensive jewelry, and countless other items. Everyday shopping for groceries, nuts and spices can be done here too, while fruits and vegetables can be found in the halls of the Crusader Hospital of St. John.

Many of the Mameluke buildings, with their recessed, semi-domed entrances, belong to the Wakf, the Moslem religious authority, and house mosques, religious schools, khans, bath-houses, fountains and tombs of notables. The Mamelukes were slaves of the Turkish-Egyptian

militia who gained independence in the region and ruled from 1250 to 1517, building many Islamic institutions in Jerusalem, especially in the Temple Mount area. Part of the Via Dolorosa is located in the Moslem Quarter.

The Hurvah Square ▲

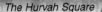

One of the Sephardi synagogues ▲
in the Jewish Quarter

The Burnt ▼
House

The Jewish Quarter

The Jewish Quarter lies along the city wall between Zion Gate and Dung Gate and was already inhabited in the time of the First Temple. Remains of a section of the city wall - the Broad Wall - built in the seventh century B.C by King Hezekiah to protect the city against the armies of Assyrian king Sennacherib, have been discovered. Recent excavations beneath the debris and ashes remaining from the Roman destruction of Jerusalem in 70 A.D. have thrown light on life in Jerusalem during the Second Temple era, revealing elegant mansions such as the Burnt House, the home of a High Priest.

However, among the most remarkable finds in the Quarter is that of part of the Cardo, the main street of the Roman-Byzantine city Aelia Capitolina, most of which lies below todays street level. The sixth century mosaic Madaba map from Jordan depicts Jerusalem at that time, showing the original Cardo

in the center of the map as a wide, elegant arcaded avenue. The Crusaders built a market there and today part of it has been restored and lined with modern tourist boutiques.

The heart of the Jewish Quarter is the cafe-lined Hurvah Square, with the remains of the Hurvah Ashkenazi synagogue. The synagogue was first built in 1701 but was burnt down. Jews from Poland started rebuilding in the 18th century though it was only completed in 1864. This impressive building was the center of Jewish life in the Holy Land, however it was blown up by the Arab Legion in 1948 and has been left a ruin. Also on the square is the oldest synagogue in Jerusalem, the Ramban synagogue founded in 1267 by Rabbi Moshe ben Nahman. Nearby are four Sephardi synagogues clustered together in a single compound, built by Jewish refugees from Spain in the 16th century. Under Jordanian rule they were used as stables, but since 1967 they have been beautifully restored.

Today, the Jewish Quarter, from which the Jews were exiled in 1948, has been rehabilitated. Conforming to the traditional style of former building, beautiful homes with courtyards and patios have been constructed as well as large Yeshivas - religious centers of learning. Among the ruins of the Quarter are those of the Nea, Emperor Justinian's church.

Remains of the Roman Cardo ▼

Remains of the Roman Cardo ▼

The Western Wall

The Western Wall was not actually a part of the Temple. Biblical Jerusalem was built on two hills: the eastern Moriah and the Ophel. Between them was a valley that has since been filled in by the debris of the destroyed Temple and was situated where the present plaza in front of the Western Wall is located. There is yet another reason why Mount Moriah has lost its hilly appearance. The Western Wall is actually a retaining wall built by Herod in 20 B.C., surrounding the entire eastern hill which was raised with fill to form a flat plateau the level of Moriah's summit. It was on this elevated plaza that the Temple stood at the time of Jesus.

Ever since the destruction of the Second Temple in 70 A.D, Jews have gathered in pilgrimage and in prayer at the Western Wall, which became known as the Wailing Wall. Its cracks are filled with hastily written prayers for the speedy recovery of the sick, for the Peace of Jerusalem and the coming of the Messiah.

"The Lord had said, In Jerusalem shall my name be for ever".
(II Chronicles 33:4)

The Western Wall Tunnels

▲ *The Hasmonean Chamber*

Only part of Herod's retaining Western Wall is visible at ground level. The rest is underground and was discovered by the British archaeologists Charles Wilson and Sir Charles Warren who, in 1867, sunk shafts along the lengths of the western and southern walls, revealing 18 courses reaching down to bedrock. Further excavations from the 1970's have uncovered remains dating from the time of King Solomon. Today, one can tour the ancient Herodian street at a depth of 50 feet below ground level, along the length of the wall. The tunnel passes stairs from the time of the Second Temple, through the remains of Wilson's Arch where a road to the Temple passed in Herodian times, a Hasmonean water tunnel, a pool and an ancient quarry.

▼*"Secret passage" - Long vault leading from the Temple Mount to Hagai Street.*

The Antonia Fortress, from the Model of Jerusalem.

The Temple, from the Model of Jerusalem.

The Basilica and Huldah's Gate within the temenos, from the Model of Jerusalem.

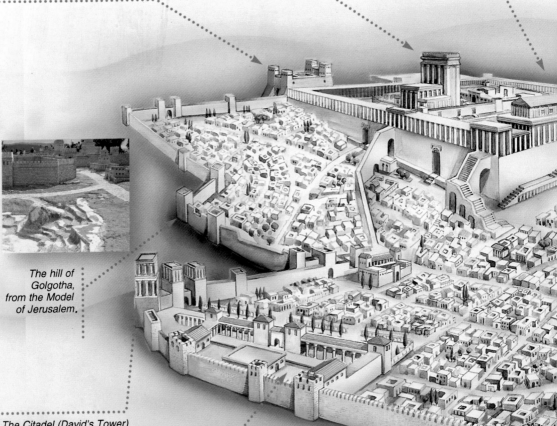

The hill of Golgotha, from the Model of Jerusalem.

The Citadel (David's Tower)

Herod's Palace, from the Model of Jerusalem.

An affluent home in the Upper City of Jerusalem.

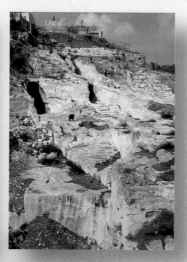

Hulda Gate and the steps leading to the Temple

Remains of channels in the City of David, quarried to deliver water to fields in the Kidron Valley.

The Pool of Siloam.

The eastern slopes of the Upper City towards the Tyropoeon Valley, an area densely occupied by smaller tightly-packed houses. From the Model of Jerusalem.

Jerusalem in the time of the Second Temple

Drawing by C. Ron

The Archaeological Park

The excavations along the southern edge of Mount Moriah have provided a rich insight into daily life in and around the Temple precincts when it was at the height of its glory. Among the many finds were a 40 feet wide paved road skirting the Temple area; a stairway 300 feet in width ascending to the Hulda Gates, stone vessels - some for holding sacrifices, a niched cornice from the Herodian period from where the priests blew the ritual trumpet which is inscribed "to the place of the trumpeting". Jesus and his disciples ascended the staircase to the Hulda Gates every time they went to the Temple.

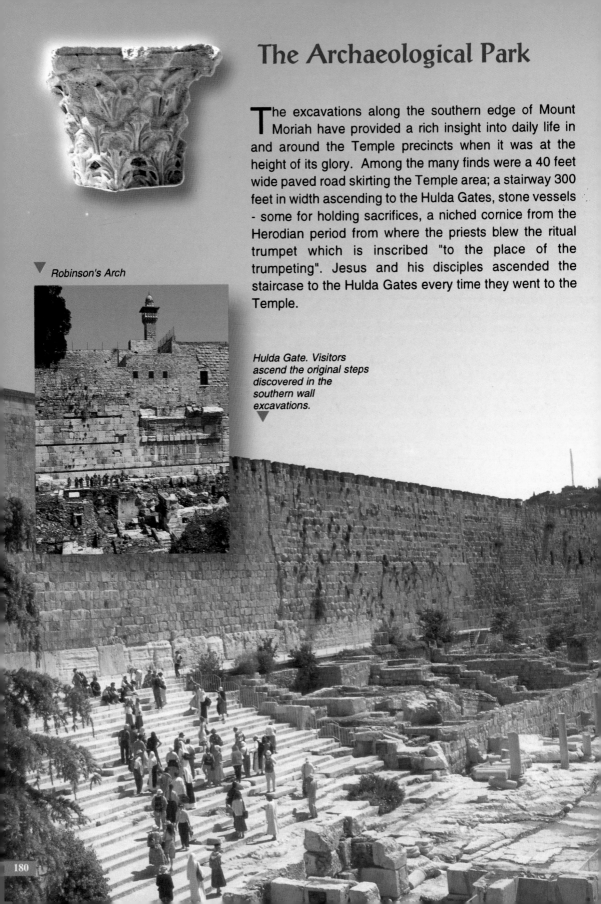

▼ *Robinson's Arch*

Hulda Gate. Visitors ascend the original steps discovered in the southern wall excavations.
▼

The Citadel
and Old City Walls

Look-out point at the Citadel

The courtyard of the Citadel

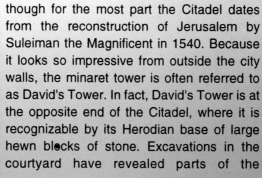
The courtyard of the Citadel

The Citadel is one of Jerusalem's oldest and most prominent landmarks. In 24 B.C., Herod built a beautiful palace south of this site. To protect his palace he constructed a series of connecting ramparts and three large towers which he named after Hippicos, a friend; Mariamne, his wife whom he murdered, and Phasael, his brother.

When Titus razed the city in 70 A.D, he was impressed by the size of these towers and left them standing as a monument to Roman valor. However, when Hadrian destroyed the city in 135 A.D., he left only part of the Phasael Tower intact, and the base of this imposing structure is visible to this day.

The present structure is built on foundations laid by the Crusaders, though for the most part the Citadel dates from the reconstruction of Jerusalem by Suleiman the Magnificent in 1540. Because it looks so impressive from outside the city walls, the minaret tower is often referred to as David's Tower. In fact, David's Tower is at the opposite end of the Citadel, where it is recognizable by its Herodian base of large hewn blocks of stone. Excavations in the courtyard have revealed parts of the

Hasmonean city wall of 100 B.C and pottery from the time of the First Monarchy.

The Citadel today houses the Museum of the History of Jerusalem and during summer months, Sound and Light performances are held in its courtyard.

The Old City walls, constructed of great blocks of grey stone, were built by the Turkish sultan Suleiman the Magnificent in 1542 on the foundations of the Roman Aelia Capitolina and the Crusader city. Measuring 2.5 miles in circumference, and varying from 30 to 60 feet in height according to the conformation of the land, the walls are pierced by seven gates: Jaffa Gate on the west, originally the starting point of the road to the most important port town; Damascus Gate, the most ornate, where the road to Damascus used to start; Zion Gate, connecting the Armenian Quarter with Mount Zion and the Lions' Gate, or St. Stephen's Gate. Other gates are the New Gate, Dung Gate, nearest to the Western Wall and through which much of the city's refuse was taken to the Kidron Valley and the Golden Gate, also called the Gate of Mercy, which has been closed for centuries and through which the Jews believe the Messiah will come.

▲ *The ramparts walk* ▼

"*Our feet shall stand within thy gates, O Jerusalem. Jerusalem is builded as a city that is compact together*"
Psalm 122:2-3

The Gates of the Old City

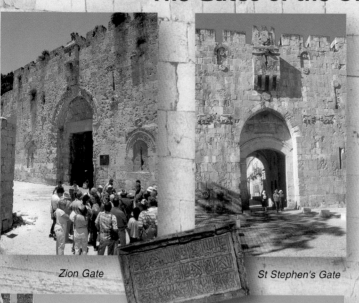

Zion Gate

St Stephen's Gate

Dung Gate

Jaffa Gate

Herod's Gate

The Golden Gate

The New Gate

Damascus Gate

Damascus Gate excavations

"Now in the place where he was crucified there was a garden: and in the garden a new sepulchre, wherein was never man laid"

John 19:41

The hill of Golgotha ▶

The Garden Tomb

Many Protestants believe that Jesus was buried in the Garden Tomb, which is set in a quiet enclosure just outside the Damascus Gate. A nearby hillock, with a Moslem cemetery on top and a broken cistern in its rocky face, bears resemblance to a skull, which could be Golgotha. In 1867, a first-century rock-hewn tomb containing two chambers was discovered near the hill. In 1882, the British General Gordon was a leading advocate for this area as a probable site of the Crucifixion and it was purchased by the Garden Tomb Association of London in 1893. The evidence for a probable site of execution near to an exceptionally large cistern and a Herodian tomb, which meets all the details mentioned in the Gospel, makes the present garden a meaningful center for Christian meditation and devotion.

▼ *Interior of the Garden Tomb*

The Russian Church of the Holy Trinity

The Municipality Complex

The New City of Jerusalem

For thousands of years, Jerusalem consisted only of the area within the walls. However, since the mid-nineteenth century, many neighborhoods have sprung up, making Jerusalem Israel's largest city today. Although Jews formed a majority of the population, they were crowded into the Jewish Quarter, a tenth of the size of the Old City. In 1860, Sir Moses Montefiore, an aristocratic British Jew, completed the construction of a row of cottages called Mishkenot Sha'ananim, "the dwelling places of the tranquil". The development was intended to draw the inhabitants out of the overcrowded hovels of the Jewish Quarter of that time to a newer, healthier life but it took another ten years until Jews were willing to brave sleeping outside the walls. The windmill, today a museum, was intended to provide employment for the

Mishkenot Sha'nanim

Zion Square

Mea Shearim street scene

The Sherover Theatre

tenants. The location chosen was on the hill west of Mount Zion, across the Valley of Hinnom, where child sacrifice was practiced in Canaanite times. At the head of the valley is the Herodian reservoir first called the Serpents' Pool, later extended by the Crusaders and then repaired by the Sultan Suleiman and renamed Sultan's Pool. It is the most popular venue for festive concerts in the summer months.

Russians have been making pilgrimages to Jerusalem

ever since the eleventh century when a monk walked all the way from Kiev to Jerusalem, carrying a silver lamp to the Church of the Holy Sepulcher. In 1860, Tsar Alexander II bought land outside the Christian Quarter of the Old City, which eventually became know as the Russian Compound. On the highest ground of the Compound is the Cathedral of the Holy Trinity with its white stone facade and 18 green domes. Nearby are the Duhovnia Russian Mission and hospices which accommodated the thousands of pilgrims who came annually. After the rise of communism, religion was outlawed and people could no longer make pilgrimages. The religious community already in Jerusalem was cut off from Russia and its members became known as the White Russian Church.

After the first break from the confining walls of the Old City, suburbs began to mushroom, each being established by groups of people with a similar background and outlook. One of the earliest, founded in 1874, is Mea Shearim, still looking much as it did a century ago. The whole community is fanatically orthodox and only Yiddish is spoken. Hebrew is observed as the language of prayer. Men wear long sidelocks and dress in long black caftans and round felt

The Mahane Yehuda Market

hats, replaced on Sabbath and holydays with the fur streimel, while the women are clothed in high-necked, long-sleeved dresses and cover their heads. Visitors are expected to dress "modestly".

Since the foundation of the State of Israel in 1948, the construction of government institutions and public buildings in the capital has gone on apace. In 1966, Israel's Parliament - the Knesset - moved to its present location, a modern building sponsored by the Rothschild family. The Knesset has many valuable works of art including three magnificent tapestries and

▲ The Knesset building

▲ Yad Vashem

Memorial to the
Freedom Fighters
of the Warsaw Ghetto,
Yad Vashem

wall and floor mosaics by Marc Chagall. The Menorah, the emblem of the State of Israel, which stands opposite the Knesset, was presented to Israel by the British Parliament. It is modeled on the seven-branched cande-labrum from the Temple which the Jewish exiles carried to Rome and depicts scenes from the history of the Jewish people.

In 1992, the Supreme Court building was completed, Israel's last public building to find a permanent home. The new Jerusalem municipality building, located near the border with Jordan between 1948- 1967, was opened in 1993.

One of the most important and most frequently visited sites of modern Jerusalem is Yad Vashem - the memorial to the six million Jews who perished in the European Holocaust during the Second World War. Archives and micro-films catalog numerous documents and other evidence relating to this catastrophe and the Hall of Remembrance, with an Eternal Light burning over human ashes from one of the crematoria, is paved with the names of the dreaded death camps. A tree-lined path leading to the museum is called the Avenue of the Righteous Gentiles, in honor of those who helped save Jews during the Holocaust.

Jerusalem's newest museum is the Bible Lands Museum, which houses a superb collection of ancient artifacts. The civilizations of the Biblical period are shown in chronological order from 6000 B.C. to 600 A.D.

▲ The Supreme Court

Bible Lands Museum ▼

The Israel Museum
& the Shrine of the Book

Opened in 1965, the Israel Museum is many-faceted, housing collections of Judaica, Art, Archaeology, the Billy Rose Sculpture Garden and - the pearl in the crown - the Shrine of the Book which contains the Dead Sea Scrolls. The white-domed exterior resembles the lid of one of the earthenware jars in which the scrolls were hidden in Qumran. Despite the fact that the Museum is relatively very new, its collections rival that of many well-established museums the world over.

Among the many gems are a seventeenth century Italian synagogue and another from Cochin, India. The Youth Wing is particularly active, with regularly changing exhibits, and the Museum has a full program of lectures, concerts and films.

◄ *Interior of the Shrine of the Book*

Model of Jerusalem

The Model of Jerusalem at the time of the Second Temple, in the grounds of the Israel Museum, was built before the reunification of the city. The 1:50 scale model was supervised by Prof. Avi-Yonah and built according to the descriptions of Josephus Flavius. Whenever excavations reveal new information, changes are made in the Model. The grandeur of the city at the time can be appreciated by viewing this replica.

Model of Jerusalem in the Second Temple period

The Chagall Windows

In 1962, the beautiful stained-glass windows by the world-famous Jewish artist, Marc Chagall, were presented to the synagogue of the Hadassah-Hebrew University Medical Center. They represent the sons of the Patriarch Jacob, from whom descended the twelves tribes of Israel, and most of the details come from Jacob's blessing of each of his sons, before his death. (Genesis 49)

The Chagall windows at the Hadassah-Hebrew University Medical Center.

▶

A painting in the Church at Emmaus depicting Jesus breaking bread while eating with Cleopas and a companion.

◀ The Byzantine Church

Emmaus

"And, behold, two of them went that same day to a village called Emmaus, which was from Jerusalem about threescore fulongs....And it came to pass, that, while they communed together and reasoned, Jesus himself drew near, and went with the. But their eyes were holden that they should not know him"

Luke 24:13.15–16

It was in Emmaus that the risen Christ appeared to two of his followers and dined in the house of Cleopas. The actual location of Emmaus is uncertain, but the Franciscans believe it to be at El-Qubeibeh, the site of a fort called Castellum Emmaus, which was discovered by the Crusaders in 1099, around 6.8 miles northwest of Jerusalem. In the twelfth century, a church, monastery and fortress were built in El-Qubeibeh and excavations have revealed that there was a settlement there at the time of Jesus. The present church was built at the beginning of the twentieth century over the remains of the Crusader church. The remains of the home of Cleopas have been incorporated into the left aisle.

The village of Amwas, ancient Nicopalis, in the Ayalon Valley has also been identified with Emmaus. Byzantine and Crusader churches were built on the site, though were later destroyed. A Mass is still held in the ruins on Easter Mondays.

ABU GOSH : On a hilltop in Abu Gosh, biblical Kirjath-Jearim, is the modern church of Our Lady of the Ark of the Covenant. This a popular venue for concerts.

◀ The Church of Emmaus (El Qubeibeh)

Bet Guvrin

The ancient cities of Maresha and Bet Guvrin are today incorporated into the Bet Guvrin National Park. Maresha is mentioned in the Bible as a city of Judah and following the invasion of Shishak of Egypt, it was fortified by Rehoboam. During the Hellenistic period, the lower city of Maresha, then called Marisa, was built by Greeks and its complex system of caves quarried. From this period there are remains of houses, a well-preserved bathroom, water cisterns and a columbarium. Some of the caves were used for burial and these are called the Sidonian burial caves after an inscription reading "chief of the Sidonians at Maresha". This city became an important economic center, but in around 113 B.C., it was conquered by the Hasmoneans and its inhabitants were forcibly converted to Judaism. The settlement declined and fell to the Parthians in 40 B.C. Thereafter, Beit Guvrin became the main city of the area and is mentioned in Josephus' writings as one of the towns captured by the Roman General Vespasian. From the time of the destruction of the Second Temple until the Bar Kochba Revolt, it was a flourishing Jewish city and its sages are mentioned in third and fourth century Jewish sources. During the Byzantine period, it was an important Christian center and remains of churches have been uncovered, including that of St. Anne which was rebuilt in the Crusader period.

A cave at Bet Guvrin

The colombarium cave

Sidonian burial cave

The Monastery of Latrun in the Ayalon Valley ▶

▼ *The "Elah" Valley*

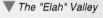

St George's
Church,
Lod

Lod & Ramla

Today known by tourists as home to Israel's Ben-Gurion International Airport, Lod, originally known as Lydda, has a long history dating back to pre-biblical times. Here St. Peter miraculously cured Aeneas the paralytic (Acts 9). Lydda is most famous as the birthplace of the martyred St. George, patron saint of England, who slayed the dragon here. The Greek Orthodox Cathedral of the Martyred St. George, built over the remains of Byzantine and Crusader churches, marks the spot where he is buried.

Ramla was built in 717 A.D. by Caliph Suleiman, the only town ever established by the Arabs in Palestine. Later fortified by the Crusaders who thought it to be the site of Aramathea, it is today a market town with a population of Arabs and Jews. The White Tower, its well-known landmark, is part of the fourteenth century White Mosque. In the town are the eighth century cisterns of St. Helena, a reservoir which, however, has no connection to St. Helena, and the Crusader cathedral of St. John, now the Great Mosque.

Ramla, partial view

The White Tower of Ramla

Lod,
the Byzantine
mosaic

Old Jaffa

From time imme-morial, Jaffa (Heb-rew for "beautiful") has been important as a port and station on the ancient trade route of "Via Maris", which connected Egypt with Mesopotamia and the north. Legend holds that the founder of Jaffa was Japhet, son of Noah. Documentary evidence goes back 3500 years to the time when, as described in the Amarna letters, the Egyptian pharoah Thutmose III conquered the town in 1468 B.C., by bringing in with him hundreds of soldiers in innocent-looking hampers.

▲ *View to the light-house from the old harbor.*

▼ *Bird's eye view of Old Jaffa.*

II Chronicles 2:16 relates how Solomon discussed his building projects with Hiram, king of Tyre, who offered: "We will cut wood out of Lebanon... and bring it in floats by sea to Joppa", for this was the Holy Land's outlet to the wide world. Jonah 1:3 tells how he "went down to Joppa, and he found a ship going to Tarshish".

Christians associate Jaffa with Peter, who restored Tabitha to life and "tarried many days with one Simon, a tanner" (Acts 9:43). Here he had his vision which led to the first preaching of the gospel of Christ to the Gentiles. The House of Simon the Tanner and St. Peter's Church recall these events.

Another legend associated with Jaffa is that of Perseus and Andromeda, daughter of the king of Jaffa. The beautiful princess was chained to a rock in the harbor to be sacrificed to the sea monster, in order to appease its wrath. Perseus saw her in her terrible plight and rescued her by slaying the monster. "Andromeda's rock" can be seen in the harbor not far from the light-house. Today, one of Jaffa's main attractions is the Artists' Quarter, with its quaint streets and workshops.

Old Jaffa with the Church of St Peter at night ▲

Old Jaffa ▲

▼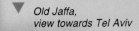
*Old Jaffa,
view towards Tel Aviv*

▲ Tel Aviv, "The city that never stops"

Tel Aviv

▲ A mall in Tel Aviv

The modern metropolis, which is today Tel Aviv, was established in 1909 by 60 Jewish families who wanted to escape the cramped living conditions of Jaffa. They bought an area of sand dunes north of Jaffa, planning to build a modern suburban quarter and called it Tel Aviv, after Tel-Abib in Babylon where the prophet Ezechiel "came to them of the captivity" (Ezechiel 3:15).

Neve Zedek Quarter ▶

▼ Tel Aviv's sky line

Center for the Performing Arts ▲

The Promenade ▲

During World War I, the Turks expelled the Jews from Tel Aviv and sent them inland, but when General Allenby rode into the town in 1918, the exiles streamed back and were quickly reinforced by floods of new immigrants. Since then, the city has grown by leaps and bounds. Today it is Israel's commercial show-case and shopping center and the hub of cultural life, known to Israelis as "the city that never stops". It is hard to believe that less than 100 years ago, the entire area was only sand dunes.

The city is bounded on the west by a long, sunny beach with a promenade reaching to Jaffa. On summer evenings, thousands of people stroll along and there are many forms of street entertainment during holiday seasons. Tel Aviv is Israel's most cosmopolitan Mediterranean city with elegant shops and a vast choice of restaurants and its inhabitants often compare it to Paris or New York. At its popular outdoor Carmel market one can buy anything from fruits, vegetables and clothes to CD's. Nearby, twice a week is the Nahalat Binyamin street market where artists engaging in every form of handiwork set up their stalls and sell to the throngs of visitors.

◄ The promenade

As the center of culture, Tel Aviv has an opera house, "The Center for the Performing Arts", a concert hall with a famous Philharmonic Orchestra, many theaters and a host of exhibition halls and museums. The Tel Aviv Museum of Art has an important collection.

Most popular is the Diaspora Museum, Bet Hatefutsot, whose aim is to present and explain the

Azrieli center ▲

Jewish way of life in the Diaspora - both day-to-day and festivals, relations of the various communities with their environment, and the return to Zion. Its exhibits include a collection of beautiful models of synagogues from all over the world, both old and new, and some of which were destroyed by the Nazis. An entire floor describes the history of Jews in the different countries in which they lived throughout the ages. Nearby is the Haaretz Museum complex which comprises Tel Qasile, once a busy Philistine town and trading post. Twelve layers of civilization have been discovered at this site including Hebrew inscriptions from the ninth century B.C. and a Philistine temple.

▼ *Tel Aviv by night*   *The Opera Mall* ▶

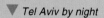

Ashdod Yam, ancient Ashdod ▲

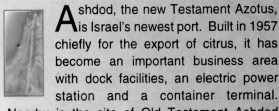

Ashdod by David Roberts 1839

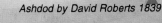

Ashdod

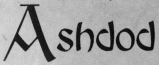

▼ *Modern Ashdod* ▲

Ashdod, the new Testament Azotus, is Israel's newest port. Built in 1957 chiefly for the export of citrus, it has become an important business area with dock facilities, an electric power station and a container terminal. Nearby is the site of Old Testament Ashdod (Joshua 15:47), one of five major Philistine cities, together with Ashkelon, Ekron, Gath and Gaza, which were interwoven with the actions of the Israelites as recorded in the book of Judges, and particularly with the wanderings of the Holy Ark. "The Philistines took the ark of God and brought it from Ebenezer unto Ashdod... and there they brought it into the house of Dagon" (I Samuel 5) with disastrous consequences.

Modern Ashkelon ▲

Ashkelon

One of the oldest and largest cities in this part of the world, 4000 years ago Ashkelon was a Canaanite city-state under Egyptian protection. Later, it became one of the five major Philistine cities. Under Greek domination, Ashkelon was an independent city, and may have been the birthplace of Herod the Great. When Herod came to power, he built palatial buildings and colonnaded walks here, adding statues and fountains. Ashkelon thrived during Roman and Byzantine times - a large synagogue from this time has been discovered - and it became one of the key coastal fortresses of the Crusaders. Ashkelon followed the same, unhappy pattern as the rest of the Crusader strongholds, for it was razed by Sultan Beybars in 1270 and lay in ruins for centuries. Today it is a residential and vacation town and many of its ancient columns, capitals and statues have been placed in its National Park.

▲ *Archaeological finds in Ashkelon's National Park* ▲

Ashkelon by David Roberts, 1839.

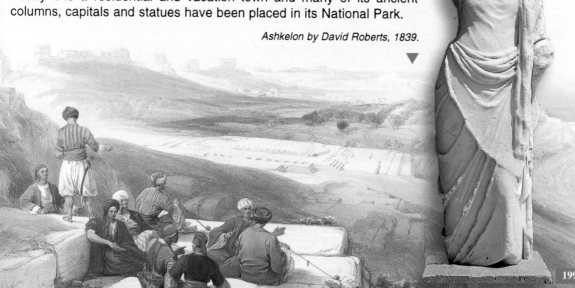

The Negev

The beautiful, majestic triangle of the Negev (meaning south) desert encompasses most of the southern part of Israel. Its landscape is varied, with mountains, canyons and wadis, which in winter are occasionally subject to flash floods. The average rainfall in the Negev is less than four inches a year, and when it does rain, the soil is unable to absorb the water. The area was, until 1948, populated mainly by the nomadic Bedouin, however although still only sparsely populated and with only one major city, Beersheba, large areas of what was once wilderness have been successfully cultivated.

The Negev is frequently mentioned in the Old Testament as 'the south' or 'south country'. In biblical times, several trade routes, including the east-west route to Egypt via Kadesh-Barnea and another linking Egypt to Arabia via Elot, intersected in the Negev. Around 2000 B.C., at the time of Abraham, the Negev was inhabited by nomadic tribes. Abraham passed through the Negev on his way from Haran to Egypt and after the destruction of Sodom and Gomorrah, he settled there. Isaac also lived in the south country when he first met Rebekkah. Before entering the Promised Land, the Israelites spied out the Negev and after it was conquered by Joshua, the region was included in the territory of Judah and Simeon, but only the northern part was settled. Here David fled to the caves of Ein Gedi and here Solomon mined copper. After the fall of Jerusalem in 587 B.C., the Negev came under the control of the Edomites, who were in turn expelled by the Nabateans. In the fourth century A.D., the Byzantines occupied many of the Nabatean settlements, expanding them and using Nabatean methods of water collection and preservation. During the following centuries, Bedouin tribes roamed the area and in 1939 the first kibbutz, Negba, was established, the start of successful Jewish settlement in the Negev.

Over the years, modern Israeli agriculturists have set up experimental farms to rediscover and improve on the Nabatean and Byzantine methods of agriculture, and to fulfil the dream of Israel's first Prime Minister, David Ben Gurion, to make the desert bloom.

Beersheba

The capital of the Negev, Beersheba, like Hebron, has age-old links with Abraham and the Patriarchs. Abraham and Abimelech "made a covenant at Beer-sheba...and Abraham planted a grove in Beer-sheba" (Gen. 21:32-33). From here he sent away his Egyptian handmaid Hagar and their son Ishmael, and here God called on him to sacrifice his son Isaac. Isaac's servants dug a well there, and "Jacob went out from Beer-sheba" (Gen. 28:10). Later it became the southernmost point of actual settlement, for Judges 20:1 describes how the "children of Israel went out, and the congregation was gathered together as one man from Dan even to Beer-sheba". At the end of the nineteenth century, the Turkish authorities half-heartedly attempted to make Beersheba their administrative center for the southern division of Palestine. Since the Israel War of Independence, it has developed from a small backwater to a flourishing city, the capital of the Negev. Among its great attractions are the Thursday morning Bedouin market and the traditional Abraham's Well. A dig on Tel Sheva has revealed cave dwellings from 4000 B.C. and a complete town from the time of the Judges. around 1200 B.C, with massive city gates, palatial mansions, roads, stores and houses, a temple and a horned stone altar.

Abraham's Well ▲

The Negev Museum ▲

Bird's eye view of Beersheba ▼

The Bedouin

The nomadic bedouin are traditionally wandering herdsmen, many of whom still live in tents in a manner reminiscent of the children of Israel in the Bible. They, too, revere Moses and many of their place-names reflect their version of the story of Exodus. The bedouin are divided into tribes, each with a chief - the Sheikh - elected by adult males to oversee their tribal interests. However, times and habits are changing and bedouin dwellings are now often huts or houses instead of tents and the automobile is ousting the all-purpose camel, although camels are still kept not only for transport, but also for their milk and cheese for food and camel-hair for clothing and shelter. Many men work in the building and tourist

▲ Coffee time

▲ Baking pita (Bedouin bread)

A Bedouin tent ▼

industries while the women work at home on bedouin arts and crafts to sell to tourists.

Hospitality is an important aspect of bedouin culture and is performed religiously, even if it means sharing the last piece of bread. Strangers are never asked questions and will immediately be offered refreshments. Honored guests will be served with the meat of a precious goat from the herd, specially slaughtered for them.

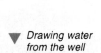

▼ Drawing water from the well

Woman churning milk in a goat-skin ▼

▼ Smoking a nargila

Avdat = The Nabateans

The Nabateans were a trading nation who had their beginnings around the fifth century B.C. and over the years grew in power and importance by controlling the caravan routes. These routes linked Gaza on the Mediterranean to Eilat on the Red Sea, extended across to Arabia, and up through Jerusalem to the lands of the north. Their capital was the "rose-red city" of Petra, now in Jordan, and they were most influential between the second century B.C. and the first century A.D when the Romans changed their status from that of an empire into a Roman province. The Nabateans retained their culture, their characteristic architecture and handicrafts. They appear to have later been Christianized and absorbed into the Byzantine regime. The basilicas on the Nabatean sites are later additions.

There were five Nabatean towns in the Negev known together as the Pentapolis - Avdat, Halutza, Shivta, Mamshit and Nitzana. Avdat, first of the Nabatean towns to be restored, is typical in its town planning, with paved streets draining into communal cisterns; well-built houses, and other communal facilities such as those for wine making and pottery-firing. The Nabatean system of water collection and storage was remarkable, making the Negev blossom, and experiments to copy their methods have been in progress since the 1950's. Inscriptions found on their sites are in Aramaic, a language similar to Hebrew. Shivta and Mamshit have also been restored.

▼ *Ruins of Avdat*

Sde Boker

Ben Gurion's Tomb

David Ben Gurion, Israel's first prime minister, chose Kibbutz Sde Boker as a place of retirement and here he and his wife are buried, overlooking the Wilderness of Zin. Ben Gurion planned a great future for the Negev, of industrial and agricultural development. His dream was to make the desert bloom and at the nearby Sde Boker College is the Desert Research Institute, where Israel's top scientists study the environment with a view to making the most of life in the desert.

In Ein Avdat National Park is the magnificent Avdat Canyon. It has sheer white cliffs and the ravine narrows as it approaches Ein Avdat, a deep translucent pool of icy water fed by a small waterfall. Further on is Ein Mor - the Bitter Pool - with a high salt content, and beyond is yet another. The oasis is inhabited by desert animals and birds.

▼ Zin Brook

▲ Ben Gurion's room

Ramon Crater

Gazelle nursing

The enormous Makhtesh Ramon, the Ramon Crater, at an elevation of about 3.280 feet, is about 25 by 5 miles, surrounded by a moonscape of mountain peaks. In the town of Mitzpeh Ramon, on the edge of the crater, is a Visitors' Center with a panoramic view of the Crater and displays of the flora, fauna and geological formations to be found there. The Crater was created by deep erosion of water and its geological layers have revealed different rock types, unique fossilized plants and footprints of dinosaurs from 200 million years ago. There is a winding road into the crater with signs along the way explaining the various rock types and formations.

At Mitzpeh Ramon is an alpaca farm, where these South American camel-like animals are raised for their wool.

▲ At the alpaca farm

▼ The Ramon Crater

Ibex ▶
(Capra Ibese
Nubiana)

◀ Ostriches
(Struthio Camelus)

Hai Bar

In an area of 8000 acres of semi-desert, a successful attempt has been made at Hai Bar to restore to the Holy Land creatures which roamed here in Biblical times. Some have been imported from abroad, mainly from the East African savannah. Hai Bar is home to various horned animals such as the ibex, which alone of all the animals has remained in the Arava valley since biblical times, oryx, addax and gazelle. There are also ostriches, wild asses and many noctural fauna such as wolves, hyaenas, foxes and the desert lynx.

▼ Addax (Addase Nasemaculatus)

▲ Somali wild asses

207

Timna Park

Views in the Timna Park ▼

▼ King Solomon's Pillars

The Timna copper mines have produced copper on and off for 6000 years. Unproven tales associate the Timna mines with King Solomon, but excavations have revealed that Timna was the earliest copper mine in the world, and was efficiently utilized around 4000 B.C., while in the fifteenth century B.C copper-mining became an important Egyptian industry.

In the shadow of the huge rocks known as Solomon's Pillars, an Egyptian temple to the goddess Hathor has been discovered, together with over 11,000 inscriptions. A Midianite shrine of about 1250 B.C., the time of Moses, was also found containing were various statuettes, notably that of a copper snake reminiscent of Numbers 21:9: "Moses made a serpent of brass and put it upon a pole". Abandoned for over 1000 years, the copper mines were re-used by the Romans until the third century A.D but neglected till modern times.

The Nature Reserve, with its awe-inspiring scenery, includes part of the ancient copper mines, an excavated Temple of Hathor and the stone "Mushroom".

Eilat

Eilat is first mentioned in Numbers 33:35, which tells how the children of Israel, on their way to Kadesh Barnea around 3300 years ago, "encamped in Ezion-gaber". I Kings 9:26 describes how "Solomon made a navy for ships at Ezion-Gaber which is beside Eloth on the shore of the Red Sea". It was probably through the thriving port of Eloth that the Queen of Sheba came on her way to Jerusalem to see Solomon. The port continued to flourish under the Kings of Judah until the great storm that apparently put an end to recorded Jewish maritime commerce in the Red Sea for 3000 years.

Called Berenice by the Egyptian Ptolemies, the port was renamed Aila by the Romans and continued to thrive under the Byzantines when it even had its own bishop. After the Muslim conquest of the seventh century it fell into decline though the Crusaders did come here. Abandoned after the second Muslim invasion, it contained nothing but a derelict police post called Um Rash-rash when the Israel Defence Forces took Eilat in March 1949. It was a desolate dry desert and water was only to be found in an oasis nine miles away. The town began to develop in 1956 after the Suez campaign when the Straits of Tiran were

▲ Water sport

▲ The Red Sea Marina ▼

Eilat's mountains ▲

opened to shipping. A new era of expansion was inaugurated after the Six Day War when Eilat became a springboard to the Sinai Peninsula.

Eilat is uniquely situated on a narrow strip of land where the mountains of Sinai and the desert of the Arava valley meet the Red Sea. Apart from its incredible all-year-round summer and constant sunshine together with magnificent views, Eilat offers the widest possible range of water sports of every kind and has excellent restaurants and plenty of nightlife. It is today Israel's most popular tourist resort, with hotels and beaches all along the shore, and has also become a paradise for sun-hungry European tourists.

General view of Eilat ▼   Camel riding ▲

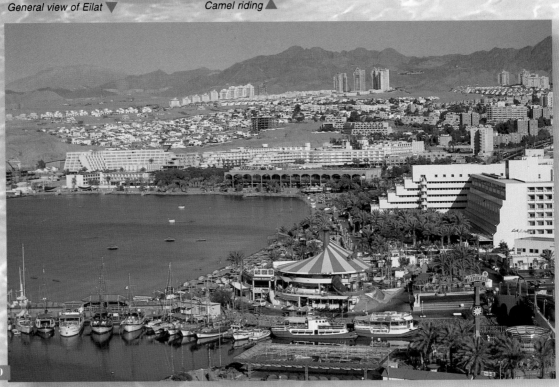

The **Dolphin Reef** was built in 1990 to enable dolphins to be kept in open captivity. The Reef is a home base for the dolphins, with an open gate which allows them to go out at will, or to stay within the enclosure. The dolphins can be observed and studied in their natural environment while their natural instincts and skills are retained, guaranteeing that should they decide to live outside the Reef, they will be able to survive and thrive like any free dolphin. A research center has been set up here and there are several on-going health care and therapy programs helping people suffering from physical or mental handicaps.

Eilat by night ▲

Bird's eye view of Eilat ▼

The Underwater Observatory

Eilat's most visited site is the remarkable Underwater Observatory - "Coral World" - which affords the visitor a unique opportunity to get acquainted with the splendor of the underwater life of the Gulf of Eilat. Here one can view the magnificent coral formations and fish, sponges and other invertebrates from large windows in the wall. There are aquaria with tropical fish, pools containing sharks, sea-turtles and stingrays and a Yellow Submarine from which one can observe the deeper coral reefs.

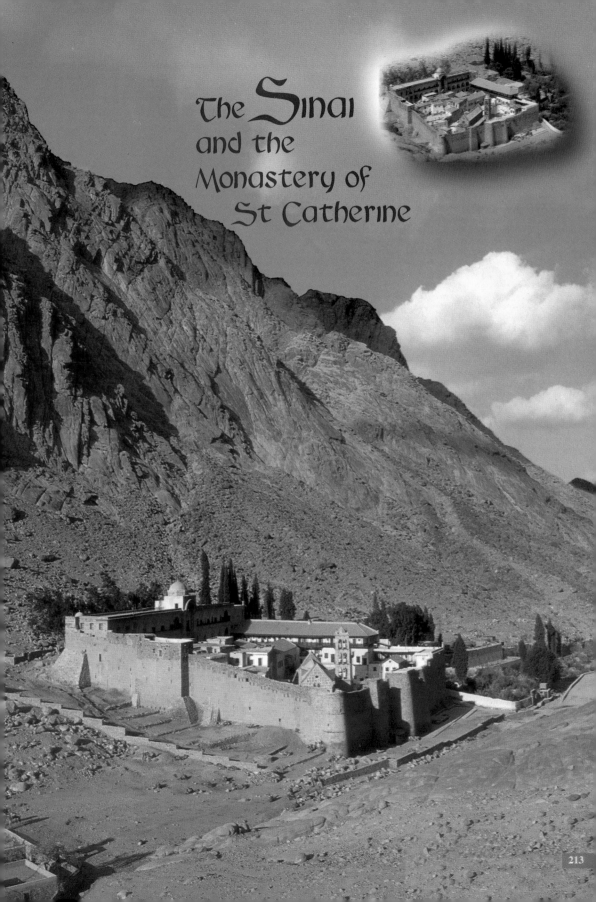

The Sinai and the Monastery of St Catherine

The Sinai desert is described in Deuteronomy 1:19 as "the great and terrible wilderness". The Children of Israel journeyed here for forty years until they were allowed into the Promised Land and it was here on Mount Sinai that Moses received the Ten Commandments which are still recognised as the foundation of religious beliefs and social behaviour. The majestic desert scenery of the peninsula with its many different colored rocks is evidence of the turbulent movement of the land which is the meeting place of the two continents of Africa and Asia. Also breathtaking is the underwater scenery of coral reefs with their marine flora and fauna.

Among the outstanding sites is Jebel Mussa - the Mount of Moses or Mount Sinai - where, tradition holds, Moses received the Tablets of the Law. Exodus 19:20 graphically describes how "the Lord came down upon Mount Sinai...and called Moses up to the top of the mount; and Moses went up". At the foot of the mountain is the Greek Orthodox Monastery of St. Catherine named for a martyred fourth

▲ 7th century icon
of Jesus Pantocrator

The skull-house

▲ Emblem of the Monastery

▼ Clock tower

214

An artist's impression of Moses with the Ten Commandments

On the top of Mt Sinai

century saint, erected on the traditional site of Moses' Burning Bush. Here Moses heard the voice of the Lord from a bush which "burned with fire, and was not consumed" (Exodus 3:2). This great fortified monastery was built by the Emperor Justinian in the sixth century, and a Greek inscription there dedicates it to him and his wife Theodosia. The Basilica of the Transfiguration, with a fine wall mosaic, is the oldest of the buildings and the library has a wealth of rare icons and manuscripts.

The ancient Egyptians sent expeditions to Sinai to bring copper and turquoise from the mines there. At Serabit el-Khadem, remains of ancient turquoise mines and of a temple to the Egyptian goddess Hathor have been found. A number of stelae, inscribed with hieroglyphics and Proto-Sinaitic scripts are still in place.

Coral Island - also known as Faro's Isle - is also of historic interest. It was occupied by the Crusaders who erected a fortress on Byzantine foundations, until taken by Saladdin.

Ruins of the temple of Hathor, Mistress of the Turquoise, at Serabit el-Khadim, Sinai.

Spectacular scenery can be found in the colorful oases of Wadi Firan, Ein Hudra and Ein Furtaga, while along the coast of the Gulf of Aqaba are many vacation resorts and villages offering water sports and diving in the magnificent coral reefs.

215

Aqaba ▲

Amman ▲

▲ Kerak
▼ Jerash

Jordan

Jordan has been a cradle of civilization since time immemorial and the country is filled with archaeological sites attesting to ancient settlement. In biblical times, todays Jordan was home to the Canaanites, Moabites, Ammonites and Edomites and other tribes inimical to the Israelites. Moses died in Moab, allowed only to see but not to enter the Promised Land. Under his successor, Joshua, the Israelites had to fight many battles in Jordan, notably one at Rabbath Ammon, now the capital city Amman. King David also defeated the Ammonites and killed the entire population. During the Hellenistic period, the area became an important trade route from Aden and Yemen to Damascus. King Herod the Great also left his mark on Jordan at Machaerus, one of the fortresses he built, where John the Baptist was later beheaded. New Testament Gadara is sometimes identified as Umm Qais which, during this period, was a large heathen city. It was in Gadara that Jesus met the men possessed by evil spirits, which he cast into a herd of swine. The Romans built Jerash, which they called Geresa, one of the cities of the Decapolis of which many remains can still be seen today.

For many hundreds of years, Jordan was beyond the realm of Western travellers, until the nineteenth century when a few intrepid travellers discovered the fascinating desert land with its castles, Petra, Jerash and Madaba and these became popular travel destinations.

The colonnaded street

Petra

Ancient Petra is traditionally biblical Sela, capital of Edom. According to legend, it was here that Moses struck the rock and drew water (Exodus 17). The Nabateans made it their capital city in the sixth century B.C. and carved the magnificent structures we see today into the rose-red colored rock. These were used as burial places and for other ritual purposes; the Nabateans were a semi-nomadic people and did not build permanent homes, so no houses or other remains survive. From Petra, the Nabateans controlled their lucrative trade routes and enjoyed centuries of prosperity. At first, they coexisted with the Roman empire, however in 106 A.D the Romans took over their city.

Petra was cut off from the West for over 1000 years: the Bedouin who lived here guarded their secret place jealously, refusing entry to outsiders. In 1812, a young Swiss explorer, Burckhardt, disguised himself as a Muslim and entered Petra, telling his suspicious guide that he had vowed to sacrifice a goat at Jebel Haroun (Mt. Aaron, where the Bedouin believe that Moses' brother died and is buried). After Burckhardt's accounts of Petra were published, the ancient city opened up to foreign travellers.

▼ The Treasury

Ed-Deir
(The Monastery)
▼

▲ *Mosaic in the Baptistry of Moses, Mt Nebo.*

Mt nebo & Madaba

It was on Mt. Nebo that Moses stood and gazed over the Promised Land that he was not allowed to enter (Deuteronomy 34) after leading his people through the desert for forty years. Located 800 meters above sea-level, Mt. Nebo commands a breathtaking view and on a clear day, the Judean hills, the Dead Sea and Jerusalem are visible. In the sixth century, a basilica was built here and numerous beautiful mosaics have been uncovered. In biblical times, many battles were fought over nearby Madaba. Spectacular mosaics and fragments from the early Christian period have been excavated. In 1898, the sixth century map of Palestine that made Madaba famous was discovered. Comprised of 2.3 million tiles, it depicts the Holy Land, naming 150 sites.

▼ *Section of the Madaba map depicting Jerusalem*

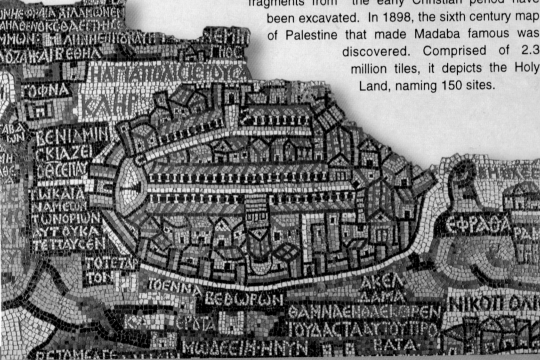

Chronological Table

CANAANITE PERIOD

❖ **c.4000-3000 B.C.**
Megiddo, Hazor and Jerusalem first built.
❖ **c.1800-1700 B.C.**
Abraham arrives in Canaan from Ur of the Chaldees in Mesopotamia.
❖ **c.1600 B.C.**
Descendants of the Patriarchs migrate to Egypt because of famine in Canaan.

ISRAELITE PERIOD

❖ **Late 13th century B.C.**
Exodus from Egypt.
❖ **13-12th centuries B.C.**
Conquest of Canaan by Israelites led by Joshua and division of Land among Twelve Tribes.
❖ **12-11th centuries B.C.**
Judges rule Israel.
❖ **c.1029-1007 B.C.**
Israel united under King Saul to combat Philistines who had invaded Canaan and established cities along coast at Gaza, Ashkelon, Ekron, Gath and Ashdod.
❖ **c.1000-968 B.C.**
King David completes the Israelite conquest ruling first from Hebron and then from Jerusalem which he had captured from the Jebusites.

FIRST TEMPLE PERIOD

❖ **c.968-928 B.C.**
Solomon builds the magnificent Temple on Mount Moriah in Jerusalem.
❖ **928 B.C.**
Following Solomon's death, division of the monarchy. The northern kingdom of Israel is ruled by Jeroboam from Shechem and the southern kingdom of Judah is ruled by Rehoboam from Jerusalem. During reigns of Ahab and later kings of both kingdoms, prophets arise protesting moral laxity and religious depravity.
❖ **722 B.C.**
Kingdom of Israel destroyed by Assyrians and the population exiled and later disappeared (The Ten Lost Tribes).

❖ **587 B.C.**
Jerusalem destroyed by the Babylonians under Nebuchadnezzar and the population of Judah exiled.

SECOND TEMPLE PERIOD

❖ **538 B.C.**
Cyrus II of Persia who had conquered most of the area issues a decree enabling Jews to return to Jerusalem and rebuild the Temple, which is completed in 515 B.C.
❖ **445 B.C.**
Nehemiah rules Judah and rebuilds the walls of Jerusalem.

HELLENISTIC PERIOD

❖ **333 B.C.**
Alexander the Great defeats the Persian Empire and sets out to conquer the world. After his sudden death in 323 B.C., his empire disintegrates. During this period the Bible is translated into Greek (the Septuagint).
❖ **167 B.C.**
The Seleucid Antiochus Epiphanes begins to Hellenize in Palestine and forbids practice of Judaism. This leads to a successful revolt headed by the Maccabees, members of the Hasmonean family. In 165, the Temple is purified and rededicated.

ROMAN PERIOD

❖ **63 B.C.**
The Romans under General Pompey enter Palestine and end Hasmonean rule.
❖ **37-6 B.C.**
Herod the Great becomes King of the Jews. He rebuilds the Temple and other monumental projects including Caesarea, Herodion and Masada.
❖ **4 B .C**
Jesus born in Bethlehem.
❖ **c.27-30 A.D**
Jesus' ministry in the Galilee.
❖ **c.29 A.D**
Jesus crucified in Jerusalem.
❖ **66-73 A.D.**
Jewish Revolt against the Romans. In 70, Jerusalem falls to Roman General Titus and the Temple is razed. Only the Western Wall survives.

- **73**
  Fall of Masada, the last Jewish stronghold.
- **132-5**
  Bar Kochba Revolt. After it has been suppressed, Hadrian destroys Jerusalem and builds Aelia Capitolina, a pagan city, in its stead.

BYZANTINE PERIOD

- **313**
  Constantine recognises Christianity, later converting himself. In 326, his mother Helena comes to the Holy Land and builds great basilicas over holy sites.
- **335**
  Consecration of the Church of the Holy Sepulcher.
- **614**
  Persian conquest of the Holy Land. Many churches and monasteries destroyed.
- **628**
  The Holy Land is recaptured by the Byzantines.
- **629**
  Emperor Heraclius enters Jerusalem and restores the Holy Cross.
- **630**
  Mohammed's Hejira ("flight") from Mecca to Medina.
- **632**
  Death of Mohammed.
- **634-8**
  Moslem conquest of the Holy Land and start of rule by the Caliphs.

CRUSADER PERIOD

- **1099**
  Crusaders conquer Jerusalem and massacre all its inhabitants. Establishment of Latin Kingdom of Jerusalem under Baldwin I.
- **1147**
  Second Crusade arrives in the Holy Land.
- **1187**
  Destruction of Crusader army by Saladin at Battle of the Horns of Hattin, and collapse of Crusader kingdom.
- **1265**
  Mamelukes, led by Sultan Beybars, reconquer the Holy Land.
- **1270**
  Final Crusade arrives and all its participants are massacred.

Mameluke period

❖ *1291*

Last Crusader stronghold at Acco taken, signalling end of Crusader kingdom.

❖ *1333*

Franciscan Order established in Jerusalem. Its members care for holy places and pilgrims.

Ottoman period

❖ *1516-1517*

Ottoman Turkish conquest of the Holy Land. Their rule continues for 400 years.

❖ *1520*

Suleiman the Magnificent (1520-66) begins spate of building including the city walls of Jerusalem and Acre.

❖ *1799*

Napoleon Bonaparte invades Palestine but does not succeed in capturing it and is forced to leave

British mandate

❖ *1917*

Palestine is taken by the British General Allenby, signalling the end of the Ottoman Empire. The Balfour Declaration promises the Jews a National Home.

State of Israel

❖ *1948*   State of Israel proclaimed.
          War of Independence.

❖ *1967*   Jerusalem is united under Israeli sovereignity.

❖ *1973*   Yom Kippur War.

❖ *1978*   Peace treaty with Egypt.

❖ *1993*   Oslo agreement with Palestinians.

❖ *1994*   Peace treaty with Jordan.

Index